The Good News About Sex

DAVID KNIGHT

Nihil Obstat:

Rev. Hilarion Kistner, O.F.M.
Rev. John J. Jennings

Imprimi Potest:

Rev. Andrew Fox, O.F.M.
Provincial

Imprimatur:

+Daniel E. Pilarczyk, V.G.
Archdiocese of Cincinnati
July 12, 1979

The *Nihil Obstat* and *Imprimatur* are a declaration that a book or pamphlet is considered to be free from doctrinal or moral error. It is not implied that those who have granted the *Nihil Obstat* and *Imprimatur* agree with the contents, opinions or statements expressed.

Cover, book design and photos by Julie Van Leeuwen.
Photo on page 88 by Chuck Debevec.

SBN 0-912228-57-1

I believe the answer [to why the Christian Gospel seems to offer youth so little positive guidance in the area of sex] . . . is that most young adults do not perceive Christian sexual ethics as "evangelical," that is, as "good news." They are not hearing the Gospel as good news and therefore they are not hearing the Gospel at all, but something else.

Harvey Cox, The Secular City

Acknowledgments

Special thanks are offered here to Sister Agnes Stretz, O.S.C., of the Monastery of St. Clare in Memphis, who typed this manuscript as fast as I could get it written and insisted that I write it as fast as she could type it.

I also thank Sister Mary Rose Bumpus, R.S.M., for testing the first version of this manuscript in her classes at Catholic High School, Knoxville, and the students and faculty of Immaculate Conception High School in Memphis for the help they gave me in working out these ideas, and other groups of students from the eighth grade through college all throughout the United States, whose response in classes and retreats is a part of these pages.

Finally, to the married people who read this manuscript and offered invaluable help, especially Mrs. Karen Hurley of St. Anthony Messenger Press, Mrs. Renny Pidgeon, and Mrs. Karen Hudgens of Memphis, I am deeply grateful.

All royalties from this book go to Birthright of Memphis.

Table of Contents

Why Another Book About Sex?
An introduction

My original intention was to write this book for young people of college and high school age who are struggling to discover sexual values and are open to moral challenge.

But as the book developed I found I was unable to write for any specific category of reader, either in content or in style. When I tried to write for teenagers I seemed to strike a false note. My style didn't sound like me—even though most of the ideas and expressions in this book were developed while talking to teenage audiences. Finally I recalled that the books we teach to the young—in English literature, for example—were not written for teenagers either.

So I have written this book as I feel it—saying what I want to say as clearly and as simply as I can. As it is written, however, I would not call it a "teenage" book. I hope it will be helpful to the young; that is my first prayer. But it should be of benefit to anyone who is looking for a deeper appreciation of sex. In particular, I hope it will help parents and teachers articulate their own experience and feelings about sex to the young. I hope it will help the married to relate more loving-ly and more sexually to each other, and the en-gaged to prepare for this.

But is this book really necessary? What excuse can there be in our times for another book about sex?

There are so many volumes on sexuality avail-able today that I feel embarrassed adding another one. And yet I am writing this book because I keep running into the need for it.

Talking to high school and college students, I find that most of what I say here is new to them. As one high school senior put it, "No one ever ex-plained sex like that to us before." I owe a great deal to the encouragement I have received from students, including those who told me quite frank-ly that the ideals I presented were too high for them to follow.

Even married couples to whom I have pre-sented the content of this book in lectures, classes and retreats tell me they have never had the mean-ing and value of sex presented to them in this way. They say it gives them a whole new perspective.

I see one article after another in the slick magazines, one book after another that is offered to young people. And as I read them my feeling is always that the best shots being scored are a near miss.

Others much more specialized than I have written about the biological, psychological and sociological aspects of sexuality. The answers to countless questionnaires have been tabulated, analyzed and reported. Statistics on teenage pregnancy, abortion and premarital sexual experience are kept up-to-date and monitored like radioactive fallout after a nuclear accident. The effects of premarital sex on later married happiness have been calculated in repeated books and articles. The data is enormous.

There are excellent books available to teach students the facts of life, both biological and psychological. And every year fresh manuals of instruction on married sex appear on the bookracks with the regularity of new leaves sprouting on the trees. Some are trashy, some serious and some sublime—but they all point to the same conclusion: There is yet a gap to be filled. People still haven't found what they are looking for in sex.

What contribution does this book hope to make?

The recognition of freedom

In July, 1977, Eunice Kennedy Shriver wrote an article for the *Washington Star* (later condensed in *Reader's Digest*, November, 1977) calling for a new emphasis on moral values in the area of sex. We are talking about teenagers, she says, as if they had no power of free choice, no ability to understand and respond to rational ideals and to arguments based on meaning and value. Society seems to take for granted that the young are nothing but chips tossed about on an uncontrollable sea of

3

interior emotions and cultural trends, and that the highest thing anyone can aim at in our sexually hyperstimulated world is to cut down the figures on pregnancy.

Short of locking the whole teenage population in their rooms, she quotes one syndicated columnist as saying, there is nothing adults can do for the young except take for granted that they will be having intercourse together and teach them how to avoid the consequences.

Our society excels in compiling data on the sociological forces that combine to herd teenagers down a common sexual path. Yet we tend to forget that these same teenagers are human persons who are free, and that many of them are intensely devoted to God. In the solutions offered to the young there is small support for the act of moral choice, little to suggest that anyone respects teenagers' ability to say no as well as yes — even to their own sexual desires — and to respond to an ideal that focuses on personal responsibility and control.

It used to be a parting joke to say to someone, "Be good — and if you can't be good, be careful!" Now it doesn't seem to enter society's mind that anyone might be good. And with an epidemic of one million teenage pregnancies a year sweeping the country, the advice about "being careful" is getting pretty grim. The joke isn't a joke anymore.

So we have turned to the great American savior: technology.

"When it comes to the problems of dealing with teenage sexuality," Mrs. Shriver writes, "people seem to throw up their hands and look for

4

some all-purpose mechanistic solution to suppress its results rather than to confront its causes. Some suggest that all pregnancies of unwed mothers below a certain age should be aborted. Others propose bringing contraceptives to all sexually active teenagers. But giving a teenage girl the Pill will not strengthen her willpower or solve her social or emotional problems. . . .None of these mechanical solutions deal with the real problem. . . ."

Why must we automatically turn to technology for the solution to our human problems? There is more to human living than biological processes and conditioned reflexes. People are more than machines. As Mrs. Shriver insists: "If we listened to our teenagers we would discover that they do have values. These values and convictions are developed through work, the family, courage, sacrifice and commitment."

So let's take a look at values.

Teaching sex as a value

The values that the young accept—even heroically—in the areas of peace and justice, helping the poor and retarded, serving as volunteer workers in slums and migrant camps, and resisting consumer manipulation are proof of their ability to accept values in the area of sex and to live by them. What young people are "thirsting for," Mrs. Shriver concludes, "is someone to teach them."

If today's society cannot teach inspiring values to its young, if the young themselves cannot respond to and reflect these values to one another, what does this say about us as a culture?

"If we do not involve our teenagers in moral

discourse," asks Mrs. Shriver, "if we do not strengthen families, if we do not add a dimension of responsibility and control to sexuality, if we do not care for those who have become pregnant and choose to keep their babies, if we can do no more than propose technological solutions to an issue that concerns human life, *what does this say about us*?"

What does it say about adult society? What does it say about the teenage culture? And, more specifically, what does it say about the Church?

A modern dilemma

In a book addressed to college students (*Living With Sex: The Student's Dilemma*), Richard Hettlinger reports "the popular, and understandable, impression that religion identifies the body with evil and sexual pleasure with sin." The Christian Churches, he says, have taken a consistently negative stance toward sex all through history.

"There are, of course," Hettlinger continues, "signs of a reaction against this distortion in ecclesiastical circles; but it will be many decades before the heritage of anti-sexualism is erased from the image of the church. Under the circumstances it is not surprising that the student, to whom sex is among the most exciting potentialities of life, regards the official codes of Christendom as meaningless."

And, in fact, he witnesses, "I myself have found very few, even among the most regular churchgoers, who regard the teaching of their church or the Bible as relevant to their sexual activity."

Hettlinger's book offers little more than its title suggests: a way of accepting sex as a problem—a dilemma in modern-day student life—and of trying to cope with it. The book doesn't develop the concept of sex as a value in itself. It seems to begin and end, in fact, with the discouraging assumption that sexual purity is unattainable, and the best a student can strive to achieve is to keep compromises within certain limits.

To whom, then, shall we look for some inspiring and positive input about sex? Does the teaching of Jesus Christ tell us anything about the positive value of sex? Does Christ teach us how to rejoice in sex and to grow through it toward the fullness of human life? Could Jesus be the "someone to teach them" that the youth of today are looking for?

Jesus, rules and values

Christianity has a long tradition of teaching the moral values of sex. Any attempt to understand the Christian stance toward sex, however, is defeated in advance if we identify moral values with a simple list of do's and don'ts.

To ask for such a list is the easy way out. But rules only draw boundaries; they do not give directions. They may keep people from going astray, but they don't lead anyone anywhere.

Jesus wanted his followers to walk alongside him, not just to string along behind him. He wanted them to see what he saw and love what he loved, to direct themselves consciously with him toward an ideal. For Jesus the goal of human existence was not that people just stay within a set of boundaries, amusing themselves harmlessly and aimlessly until death like children secure in a playpen, waiting for their parents' return.

The one thing Jesus refused to do was give rules that people could substitute for making their own the attitudes and values of God. Christ preached a religion of interior convictions and goals. He came to share with us the mind and heart of God. If we respond to him it must be with our minds and hearts, and with a sense of mission.

When people are motivated from within by something they understand and believe in, they are challenged to become saints and heroes. But when people have nothing more than a set of rules to abide by, they are automatically reduced to the psychological attitude of little children. Nothing more is expected of them than to keep out of trouble.

To discuss sex in terms of rules alone, then, is inevitably to give one another the impression that sex is nothing but a child's game, an aimless kind of amusement in which anything goes so long as everyone enjoys it and nobody gets hurt.

This is exactly what I want to avoid.

Moral teaching about sex must be based on the value of sex itself. Our real reason for respecting sex should be that we understand it and love it.

The integral value of sex

But what is the value in sex? And how many people—from one end of the moral spectrum to the other—have been able to say anything very deep or intelligent about it?

Sex is for pleasure. Sex is for procreation. Sex is somehow the expression of love. And sex is supposed to be a great, depth-charging experience of mutual self-discovery.

But what, precisely, is going on—on the whole human level—when two people engage authentically in sex? What gives sex its meaning and value?

And does the deep experience of sex have anything to do with the understanding and free choice of the people who engage in it? Or is human sexual fulfillment just a mechanistic result of using the proper techniques and having the right kind of body? Does it depend simply on the happenstance of encountering that perfect other to whom one's psyche reacts almost chemically, and who has the power to flip all one's switches to "go"?

Can we look to the teaching of Jesus Christ for answers to questions like these?

The way into orbit

If Jesus really is, as we proclaim him to be, the way and the truth of human living—the Way, the Truth, and the Life—and if sex is an integral part of human living, then the "good news" of the gospel must contain some good news about sex. And that good news must be inseparable from the good news about us and about our relationship with God.

This book is based on the conviction that sex does have meaning and value and that our Christian tradition has much to say about this meaning and value, even though we often do a poor job of explaining it. The good news about sex is really just an integral part of the good news about us. We need a Christian understanding of ourselves, therefore, in order to explain the meaning and value

10

that sex has in itself as a fully human act in a world of revelation and grace.

Sex is not just a physical or an emotional reality. It is not just a moral question either. Sex is a human experience. And as such it takes place on all the levels of human life—physical, cultural, personal and spiritual.

Sex is a four-stage rocket. If it doesn't fire on every level, it never gets into orbit. But for sex to be the richly human experience it is meant to be, the people who engage in it must know how to live their lives—and express their lives sexually—on all four of these levels of human existence.

That is why this book begins with an explanation, not of sex, but of the human person. The value of this book lies in keeping things together. It presents sex not as one part of being human that can be isolated from the rest, but precisely as an experience of being whole. And it presents Jesus Christ as the teacher of life in its wholeness.

Only when sex is an experience of being whole is sex authentically what it is meant to be.

Part I:
The Good News About People

This is a book about sexuality, but it begins by talking about people. Sexual behavior is something persons do. The way we think about ourselves as persons, then, has a lot to do with the way we think about sex.

In order to understand the good news about sex—on all its levels—we have to understand the good news about us—on all the levels of life that are open to us as human persons.

Part I of this book helps us to be aware of ourselves and to evaluate ourselves in the light of three questions: *What* are we? *Who* are we? *Why* are we?

These questions invite us to focus on our *nature* (the *what*), our *person* (the *who*), and our *destiny* (the *why*). And the answers which emerge help us to see ourselves as *created* (our *what*), as *self-creating (*our *who)*, and as *called (*our *why)*.

These questions show us life on four levels: the physical, the cultural, the personal and the graced or transcendent level of participation in the life of God. And they invite us to live on all four.

Part II will deal with sexuality on each of these four levels. That is why these first chapters, although they do not deal with sex directly, are the foundation for all the rest.

1.

'What,' 'Who' and 'Why'

Three ways of looking at people

One of the first questions people have to face in any relationship is the *level* on which they choose to deal with one another.

A dating arrangement can be "just physical," for example. Hardly anyone would choose to relate on that level alone.

But two people's relationship on a date might go beyond the physical without really getting personal. It might be restricted—by mutual consent—to a level of cultural game-playing. Both parties might choose to enjoy each other simply as masculine and feminine personalities with whatever exciting differences male and female roles offer.

For example, a young man making a casual date may be looking only for a girl who knows how to dress, dance, fix her hair and flatter his ego by keeping him talking about himself and who is willing to be physically warm and affectionate.

And many young women, too, are not eager to get into deeply personal relationships when they go out. Some dates are just for fun, and all they ask of the boy is that he be pleasant and enjoyable. They just want to have a good time.

Without condemning this level of relationship—because people are free to be as deep or as superficial with one another as they please—we have to recognize that what we are dealing with here is the basic choice of whether to relate to another as a *what* or as a *who*.

"What" we are

What we are means primarily what we are *able to do*. *Who* we are means the kind of person we *choose to be*. Our "what" refers to our natural endowments, whether physical, intellectual or social. Looks, physique, talents, social charm or personality are all included in what we are.

We relate to the *what* of another person when we treat him or her as an object, when we use the other for what he or she has to offer.

If this sounds like a despicable thing to do, let us remember that most business relationships are explicitly geared to remain on this level, and probably most social relationships are meant to be kept there too.

People who hire other people are not primarily interested in *who* the other person is; they want to know *what* he or she can do. People presenting themselves to be hired are offering themselves to be used, and they themselves use their jobs and their employers' talents for the purpose of making a living. In business relationships people often consider it unwise to be personally involved with each other. And many business associates who mix socially do so with the unspoken understanding that entrance into another's personal life will be by invitation only. Etiquette respects rules of distance.

Some will not play by these rules, of course. My father once stopped seeing an acquaintance of his because, as he explained it to me, "Our relationship was based on nothing but bridge."

But the choice to relate primarily to the *what* of other people—to associate with them, work with them, or even be nice to them because of what they can do for us—must be recognized as a common human option. This is what people do. And if we are honest with ourselves, we will recognize that we do it too.

This way of relating is selfish only if we are not willing to be used as much as we use. If what we give to others satisfies their needs as much as they satisfy ours, then the relationship is to everyone's advantage. It is mutually beneficial, whether it aims at the depths of personal encounter or not.

But we should be conscious of the level we are on, and be sure that we want to remain on that level.

On a date, two people relating on the level of *what* should not pretend it is more than this. It is one thing for people to enjoy going out together, to enjoy each other's company, to have a good time at a party. It is another thing to speak of personal relationship or involvement.

To know the other as a *person*—to know *who* the other is—includes a lot more than just enjoying his or her company. And many young people—even up to the day they are married—fail to get to this level. Some are hardly aware it exists.

The reason why many of us fail to go deeper in our relationships with others is that we do not go that deep in our understanding of ourselves. Very often we are conscious of ourselves only on the level of what we are able to do. We think of ourselves almost exclusively in terms of our physical and mental abilities, our personalities or charm, and the record of our accomplishments.

Were you ever asked to introduce yourself to a group by telling three things about yourself? What did you say? Or what would you say?

On the high school level, almost all the young people I have seen do this exercise described themselves in terms of *what* they were:

"I am 17 years old; I am a senior in high school and I like basketball."

"I come from West Bank, Illinois; I have two brothers and three sisters, and I enjoy riding horseback."

At professional lunches and club meetings businessmen introduce themselves by describing the work they do. Teachers tell what they teach. Mothers say how many children they have. Guest lecturers are launched by someone who tells how many books they have written. Athletes are presented as athletes. And when the awards are given out at the end of a school year, they are given for *what* people have done, not for *who* they have become.

What, then, does it mean to speak of ourselves or of others in terms of *who*?

"Who" is a question of choice

Most people are familiar with the story of Jill Kinmont as told in the book *A Long Way Up* and in the movie *The Other Side of the Mountain.*

Jill was training to be an Olympic ski champion. And she had a chance; she was good. But a tragic fall on the mountain left her paralyzed from the shoulders down. For life.

She was a *what*-oriented person. She saw her value in terms of what she could do. Happiness for her was skiing, and being good at it. When she learned that she could never ski again, it was as if the bottom of her heart had fallen out. Then her fiance walked out on her. She wanted to die.

It was another friend who changed her mind. He taught her that her real value was in herself: not in what she could do but in how she chose to respond to life.

Gradually she changed her attitude and took an entirely different stance toward what had happened to her on the mountain. To all those who know her story, her name has come to mean not "Olympic ski champion" but "heroic response to life."

She changed the loss of her *what* into the creation of her *who.* She became a *person.* And this was a free choice.

To speak of *who* another person is means to speak of his or her choices. A human person is not determined by *what* is given—the physical and mental equipment—but by how he or she chooses to work with that equipment.

We describe ourselves as persons—as *who* we

are—when we talk about the goals we have freely chosen to make our own in life and about the means we are willing to use in order to attain our goals. What determines us as persons are the ideals to which we choose to respond, the attitudes and values we freely and consciously adopt, the way we choose to relate to other things and persons on earth, the way we choose to relate to God.

It is true to say that God creates *what* we are, our human natures; but we create *who* we are. It is we who create ourselves as persons.

God works with us on this, of course. We will see later that no one alone creates himself or herself as a person. It is in responding to other persons—through relationships—that each of us becomes the person, the *who*, that he or she desires to be.

The level of "why"

And God is one of the persons to whom we can respond. He offers himself to us as a person we can know and love and have as a friend. He invites us to enter into personal relationship with him, and to form ourselves creatively as persons through a life of interaction with him.

In fact, this is why we were made. To know God and love him is our destiny.

Our response to this invitation from God is the most basic choice we make. It has more than anything else to do with determining who we are, who we will be, what our names will mean for all eternity.

Free persons do not have their destiny imposed on them. It is offered to them to choose or reject. We can create ourselves as persons either in responding to God as our destiny, or in refusing to respond. The choice we finally make determines, more basically than anything else, who we have chosen to be.

There are, then, these three basic questions we can ask about ourselves: *What* are we? *Who* are we? *Why* are we? To really understand ourselves, we have to ask all three.

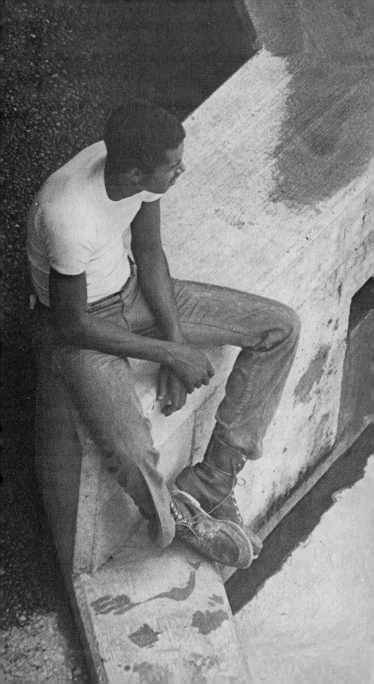

2.

A 'What' or a 'Who'?

Two ways of evaluating ourselves

Every human being, of course, is both a *what* and a *who*—a human nature and a human person. But all human beings are not equally aware of themselves as nature and as person. Some people think of themselves almost exclusively in terms of nature, in terms of what they can do. Others think of themselves almost entirely in terms of person, in terms of their interior attitudes, values and choices.

The ideal is to give full value to both aspects of our being, to develop on the level of nature and of person at the same time. But the truth, probably, is that we are so much in the habit of emphasizing one side of our personalities that we almost lose sight of the other. Or perhaps we are very aware of ourselves both as a nature able to perform and as a person able to choose, but when we relate to others, we communicate cne side of ourselves much more clearly than the other.

It may also be that, although we think of ourselves as persons, we evaluate ourselves only in terms of nature. We may be crossing our wires and thinking that our value as persons depends on what we are able to *do*.

Our fundamental realization of our self-worth is greatly influenced by our perceptions of ourselves as *what* or *who*. *What*-conscious people and *who*-conscious people have very different notions about human value, perfection and happiness.

A question of values

To think of ourselves in terms of *what* means that we measure our perfection as human beings by how well we perform, how well we function with our physical, mental and moral equipment.

By this standard, someone who judges that his or her body—or character—is not all it should be will feel inferior. Someone who can't compete physically, intellectually or socially will think of himself or herself as a second-rate human.

And, for the same reason, people who think of themselves in terms of *what they are* will put a lot of time and energy into developing *what they can do*. They will work on physical fitness and appearance, on intellectual studies and psychological development, on acquiring social finesse and on developing their skills and talents.

People who think in terms of *what* will want to be seen—by themselves and others—as beautiful, athletic, strong, musical, artistic, intellectual, entertaining, or something else that speaks of well-functioning, well-developed human equipment.

These people will seek happiness through achievement and experiences, through self-discipline and pleasure, through *using* their human equipment in ways that are effective and enjoyable. *What*-conscious people see their value in terms of what they can do. They find perfection and happiness in doing it well and receiving the recognition that comes from achievement.

Other people think primarily in terms of *who* they are. They think of themselves less in terms of *nature* than in terms of *person*.

They know that they have natures, of course, whose design and purposes they have to respect, develop and use. They find pleasure in exercise and achievement, just like anyone else. They recognize the need and value of self-discipline.

But *who*-oriented people are very conscious that there is much more to human beings than their natures—and that *who they make themselves as persons* is much more important than *what they find* (or even develop) *in themselves as natures*.

For them, a person's value is defined not in what one can do, but in how one *chooses to respond*. For them, human value consists ultimately not in physical or intellectual ability, but in response-ability.

This is not to say that it makes no difference to them whether they perform well or not. They know that part of a good response to life is to develop one's talents, to try to perform as well as one can, physically, intellectually and every other way. A human response to life cannot ignore the capacity of human nature for great deeds or the need for heroic service and accomplishment.

But *who*-oriented people just do not identify personal value with success. For them perfection consists not in performing well, but in responding to a challenge to the best of one's ability.

They look for happiness, not through doing, but through choosing. The main thing for them is not what one accomplishes, but what one becomes—what one creates oneself to be—in the act of trying to accomplish.

Accomplishments, after all, do not endure very long. Persons are forever.

For *who*-conscious people, if they are consistent, nothing in life can be really frustrating. No matter what happens, they can turn it to good by responding in a way that is loving, courageous, beautiful. Their value is not in what they have, or in what they can do, or in how other people relate to them, but in the way they respond—and in the capacity they know they have to respond even better in the future.

As one college student explained it to me: "Every choice you have to make in life is like an exam; you either pass it or you fail it. But if you fail it, God gives you a make-up test right away. The make-up test is how you accept the failure."

Performance vs. ideals

Many people struggle with guilt. *What*-oriented people think that because they fail a lot—not only in physical and mental performance, but even in moral choices—they are not good. And *who*-oriented persons think that, because they are often unable to choose what they know they should choose—and deep down really want to choose—

they must be fundamentally "bad" persons.

This is to miss the point. What determines our value as persons is not just the choices we make, but the choices we *want* to make. The ideal we love and strive for—even though we fail again and again to attain it—often says more about who we are as persons than the ideal we actually achieve.

Many years ago while I was still a seminarian, a French priest who was the chaplain of an artist colony in Zurich conducted a retreat. "I know a girl in Zurich," he told us, "who has been married five times and at present is living with three men at the same time."

Then he added: "She is the purest soul I ever met."

My instant reaction to this was, "Now I've heard it all! Only a Frenchman could say a thing like that!"

Today, however, I think I could echo his words.

Suppose you knew a girl who left home when she was 15—for whatever reason: difficulties with her parents, trouble with school, a love affair with a boy, anything. Suppose she found herself a few months later stranded in a big city, deceived by a pimp, enticed into prostitution, and unable to find her way out of it all.

Let us say, for the sake of argument, that day after day, night after night, she has intercourse with a whole succession of men. And let us say she hates it. Suppose that through every act of giving her body to be used by another, she comes to long more and more deeply for purity, for a way to experience herself as whole and entire again.

She may not know how to escape her situation. Fear may keep her there, or ignorance. Or just the paralysis of not knowing concretely where to turn. But in the measure that she begins to love and long for purity, for her integrity as a person, *she is pure.*

There is a difference between performance and personal ideals. Even the purest moral performance is not always a proof of ideals, any more than the worst moral performance is proof that a person does not care. When it comes to judging the reality of *who* a person is, one has to consider the heart.

And Jesus taught us that none of us can read the heart of another. Therefore we cannot judge.

It is only ourselves, our own hearts, that we can judge. And more often than not, we do not do a very good job of that either. Not, primarily, because we are always too easy on ourselves; sometimes we judge ourselves much harder than anyone else. Rather, we judge inadequately because we base our judgment on our performance rather than on our ideals. Or it might be that we mistake feelings, desires and temptations for the free response of our hearts.

If we judge ourselves by our performance, or by what goes on inside of us independently of our free choice, we are placing our value as persons, not in the *who* we choose to be, but in the *what* of our actual performance.

There is a big difference.

Right, wrong or guilty?

Very often in discussing moral issues, we confuse what is right and wrong with whether or not a person is guilty.

A teacher can talk about whether or not an action or a particular way of behaving is right or wrong in itself. But this does not as yet say anything about whether a person who has acted or behaved that way is personally guilty of sin.

Many things can dispose a person to do what is bad. Many people get into the habit of doing something they shouldn't long before they realize there is anything wrong with it. Then habit makes it difficult to stop. And many more people behave in a way they know is wrong without any appreciation of *how* wrong it is or how damaging to themselves and others.

A freshman in college, driving 50 miles an hour in a residential district, kills a three-year-old child who toddles into the street in front of him. A high school girl gets pregnant, is advised by her kindly doctor to "terminate the pregnancy," and in her confusion and emotional panic has an abortion.

A few years later, when both are experienced enough to realize what they did, they begin to feel terrible guilt. They think they are guilty of murder.

A counselor, in order to rid them of guilt feelings, might tell them, "Oh, there is nothing really that wrong with speeding. It was just unfortunate the child happened to be there"; or "Well, you know, a fetus in the womb is not really human life; it is just a piece of tissue." Such counseling makes a fundamental mistake: In order to relieve a person of a false sense of guilt, the reality of objective evil, of objective wrong, is denied.

A teacher would make the same mistake if he or she said that because speeding and abortion are wrong, the persons who do these things are also automatically evil.

We all do, and have done, things that are bad. And we have all been personally guilty at times. But we cannot measure how guilty we are by how bad an action is or is not in itself. It is not as simple as that. And besides, guilt is removed by forgiveness, not by denying it is there.

The way we identify or handle guilt in our lives will depend a great deal on whether we are most conscious of ourselves as *what* we are or as *who* we are.

Which am I?

Now let us ask the question again—personally: Which way of looking at self is most characteristic of my personality? Do I think of myself mostly as a *what* or as a *who*? How do my friends relate to me? And how do I relate to them?

Those of you involved in dating situations can specify the questions like this: What do you do on a date? Do you "perform" in the way that a "cute girl" or a "neat guy" is supposed to perform? Do you play a role? Do you try to project an image of yourself that invites people to respond to your physical characteristics, your intellectual ability, your social charm?

Or do you let your true self be known—your real attitudes and values; your true feelings; your deepest hopes and fears, aspirations and desires; the stance you have freely chosen to take toward life, toward other persons, toward God?

31

What does the person you date seem to want from you? To know you better as you really are? To know how you really think and feel, what you believe in, what your ideals are? Does he or she respond to who you are?

Or does he or she just want a good time, an entertaining few hours, a feeling of intimacy, a little sexual excitement? Do you feel a pressure to downplay your ideals, your beliefs, in order to please the other person?

The way you relate to others will have a great deal to do with the image you form of yourself.

If another person treats you like an object, you will be disposed to think of yourself as an object.

If another person is only interested in how you perform, you may tend to judge yourself by the way you perform. And if you just perform to please another, you lose yourself in the process.

When another person relates to us on the level of who we are, is interested in knowing our deepest thoughts and ideals, and respects them, then we will be helped to discover the kind of person we really want to be and to become authentically ourselves.

It is up to us, however, to invite the level of relationship we desire. If we only come across on the level of *what* we are, we can hardly expect the other person to relate to us as a *who*. Most people bat where the ball is pitched.

A matter of choice

What we have seen in this chapter is that human beings are both *who* and *what*, both natures and persons. We can think of ourselves—and relate to others—both in terms of what we are—what we can do—and in terms of who we are—who we choose to be.

Both areas of our being are important. But we have to choose which side of ourselves is most important; whether we will place our value, our perfection or fulfillment, our happiness in *what* we are or in *who* we are; in what we can *do*, or in how we choose to *respond*.

And in every human relationship we have to decide which part of ourselves we will present to the other—and in which part another is really interested.

The ideal is to be our whole selves for everybody, of course; to be both *what* and *who*, both nature and person in all of our relationships. And it can be done—if this is what the other person really wants; if he or she respects and is interested in us as persons as much as he or she desires to interact with our natures and to enjoy what we can do.

3.

Life Is a Four-Stage Rocket

*The physical, cultural, personal and
transcendent levels of life*

The first step in becoming a person is to know
what we have to work with. And human life is
offered on four levels: the physical, the cultural,
the personal, and on another level which for the
moment we will call the transcendent.

Not to know that one of these levels exists, or
not to develop it, is to miss out on all the opportunities for the fullness of living which that level
offers. To live life in its fullness, however, is a value
so great that Jesus Christ described his whole mission on earth in these terms:

I came
that they might have life
and have it to the full. (John 10:10)

So we need to take a close look at each of
these levels. The first two are mostly concerned

with *what* we are. The second two involve our *who* and our *why*.

The physical level

The first level is the level of our physical health and experience. It is the level of body.

This is the level we start with when we try to describe another: face, height, color of eyes and hair, figure and build, weight and muscular development; what another person looks like.

It is also, perhaps, the level we are most immediately aware of in our own lives. It is the level of sense experience: what we see, taste, hear, feel, smell; whether we are feeling healthy or sick, tired or full of energy, satisfied or restless with physical desires.

It is also the first level we think of when we ask, "Am I alive?" After all, if your body doesn't work, you are dead.

But if the only level of life we had were physical, life would not be worth living. Suppose someone were brought up from infancy as a laboratory experiment—never talked to, never taught to speak, to read, to play games, to work, or to do anything else that people do; just raised in laboratory isolation as a perfect physical specimen with no contact at all with any other person. Would that be a life we call human?

To be human, life must include a second level: the cultural.

The cultural level

The cultural level of life is the level of learned behavior. Everything we have learned from other human beings, from growing up in human society—this is what we mean by "culture."

This is the level of charm or of personality: all the pleasant—or unpleasant—ways of talking, laughing, joking, smiling, gesturing and game-playing that make up a person's mannerisms or style.

All the little tricks learned from a peer group—the way we dress, wear our hair, the slang we use, the little ways of acting that say to others we are "with it"—all these are what we mean by culture.

On the cultural level people play roles and project images to one another. And much of this is good—even necessary. The receptionist who smiles at people in an office is playing a role. And life is more pleasant for everyone because she does. If she accepts the role interiorly, she may even become a more loving person because of that role.

When young men and women date each other both are playing certain cultural roles. This is part of what makes the date exciting.

There are delightful cultural differences between men and women that make each sex attractive to the other independently of biological characteristics. The personalities of boys and girls, of men and women, are formed by the culture—and perhaps by more than the culture—to be complementary to each other.

And this is a good thing. The problem is not with culture or cultural role but in being *restricted* to it.

If a man and a woman do not relate to each other on levels other than the physical and the cultural, they will not know each other as persons. They can have a lot of fun interacting with one another culturally. But a relationship on this level is superficial, and its possibilities are soon exhausted. Cultural differences between men and women can enrich a relationship, a marriage, but they cannot make it rich enough to survive.

What makes the mystery of a man or woman inexhaustible to the other is something more than physical and cultural complementarity. It is the mystery of a unique, individual person characterized by a specific culture and physically expressed through a particular body.

How many people—of either sex—do we know on any level deeper than the physical and the cultural? How many friends do we have whose deepest levels of thought and desire are known to us? Do we know what our friends are looking for in life? What goal is most important to them? What means they think appropriate to achieve it? What actions in their lives they consider wrong, and how they feel when they do them? What their real ideals are? What they love and fear? What they base their security on? What real image they have of themselves? How they relate to God?

This is the *personal* level of life.

The personal level

I was once in a car with a group of college students when someone asked, "What do you think of teenage marriages?"

There was a long silence; then someone answered, "What do you mean by a 'teenager'? I mean, there are people in their 40's who are still teenagers in development, and there are people under 20 who are more mature than many adults."

"Well," the young man answered, "I'm 19, and I'm engaged to this girl who is also 19. I'm just wondering what you think about it."

So people started asking questions, and the answers were interesting: He had known the girl only a year. When he met her she wasn't going to church at all, although he was. But since then she had started.

"Why did she start going?" someone asked.

"I don't know; because I was, I guess," he replied.

"After you are married will you both be going to church or not? And how will you raise the children?"

"I guess we'll do whatever I decide" was his response.

"What does she like to do?" another questioned.

"The same things I do," he answered, and he offered this explanation: "Last Christmas when I came home for the holidays, she had all these things planned for us to do. But I didn't like any of them. So she just said, 'What do you want to do?' And we did that."

It doesn't take much insight to see that this boy did not have the picture. He did not know anything at all about the girl he was dating—not on the personal level, anyway. And he was in a dream world if he thought she was going to spend the rest of her life just being whatever he wanted her to be.

We know someone on the personal level when we know what his or her real goals are in life; when we know a person's real beliefs and ideals; when we know what another person cries about at night.

This is the level of relationship a person needs to reach with another before making a commitment to spend the rest of life with that person in marriage.

We are not ready to make such a commitment to another, however, until we know ourselves on this level—until we consciously enter into the personal level of our own existence.

If we do things just because everybody else is doing them, we are not yet fully persons—whether what we do is good, bad or inconsequential. If we are striving for a goal—whether it is money, success, physical beauty, athletic accomplishment, intellectual achievement, popularity or moral perfection—just because that is the goal everyone around us takes for granted as something to be desired, we have not yet become aware of the personal level of our own life.

We are fully persons when we have consciously and firmly taken possession of our own freedom and started using it to create ourselves in the direction we choose to grow in. Only such persons are ready to give themselves to another; only such persons are ready to choose another as partner in the lifelong process of growing together which is marriage.

And only on this level of mutual interaction and love can a marriage survive.

The transcendent level

When we get to the personal level of life we have gone, it would seem, about as deep as one can go. Once someone has become authentically and consciously a person, what further level is left?

What more is there to become?

If we look at human life from a purely psychological point of view, the human journey stops at personhood. To be oneself, to become a person with full and conscious responsibility for one's own life: this is the ultimate level of existence. Everything else happens from there.

For the Christian, however, there is still another level: the level which we have called *transcendent* because it transcends—goes beyond—the level of human life and existence entirely. Transcendent really means *beyond everything created*—literally "out of this world."

Strictly speaking, only God is transcendent. And for humans to live on the transcendent level is to live on a level that belongs to God alone. It is to break out of the limits of created existence—to go beyond, to transcend not just one's personal limitations, but the limitations and levels of human life itself.

This means getting into orbit.

Life is a four-stage rocket. It takes all four stages to put you into orbit, and you can't get there by living on the first three levels alone.

The person who lives just on the physical, cultural and personal levels misses the authentic fullness of life, because the fullness of life for human beings is not a level of human life at all. It is a human sharing in the life that is proper to God.

In other words, we don't really know what it is to live until we experience living like God. We have to get into *his* orbit before we are really in our own.

Some Eastern religions speak of this as if it

41

were just a matter of technique—something people can achieve by their own efforts. They encourage people to "get in touch" with the "divine element" in their own being by following certain ascetical practices—such as meditation, chanting, a diet of natural foods—as means of arriving at a higher state of consciousness.

Our purpose here is not a discussion of comparative religions. God, who called the three Magi out of the East by signaling to them through a star (Matthew 2:1-12) can bring people of every culture and religion to his Son through a variety of messengers and means. Anything good people do with an honest desire to know God, he blesses.

Our purpose is to explain what Christians mean by the transcendent level of life, a sharing in the life of God. Basically this means knowing and loving as he does; it means thinking God's thoughts and having God's desires. It means enjoying life on his level.

When the gurus and the swamis talk about a transformation of consciousness, this sounds very new and exciting—like something we have never experienced, something we do not understand. But when Christians talk about the life of grace, it doesn't turn us on at all. We just take for granted we have been experiencing grace all our lives; and we presume that we understand it.

But that is precisely what the transcendent level of life is—it is grace: a sharing in God's own life.

This experience of the life of grace should not be confused with some simple, evangelistic fervor. The life of grace is a life that itself has many levels.

These levels have been variously explained by saints and mystical writers as the "three ways" of the spiritual life (purgative, illuminative and unitive), the "seven mansions" of St. Teresa's *Interior Castle*, the "dark nights" of St. John of the Cross' *Ascent of Mount Carmel*, and so on. The literature is there for those who would like to pursue the subject.

The life of grace is a mystery—one we never fully comprehend. But this is what the good news of the gospel really is: Jesus has come to lead us to a level of life and experience that is uniquely and exclusively God's level.

That is why the early Christians called Jesus the "Master of the Way." He is the one who leads and guides his followers to the experience of life as God really offers it—life in its fullness.

This fullness of life extends to our sexual lives as well. In this book, which deals with the good news about sex, we will try to show how Jesus— the "Master of the Way"—leads us to a fullness of experience in sex that is not only human but divine. It is through the experience of sex on this level that we discover what the "breadth and length and height and depth" of sexual joy can be.

4.

The Truth Shall Make You Free
Four steps to freedom

Each successive level of life we have described is a step toward greater freedom.

Life on the level of pure, physical spontaneity is not freedom; it is animality. Purely spontaneous people eat when they are hungry, drink according to their desire, let passion dominate their sex life, run away when they are afraid, lash out at others when they are angry, stop to rest whenever they are tired, and quit when they are discouraged. They are the slaves of physical appetites, psychological drives and uncontrolled emotions. Their lives are characterized by the immaturity of children.

Civilization and freedom

The cultural level of life, "civilization," is a step upwards in freedom. It brings deliverance from uncontrolled physical and emotional drives and the attainment of a more rational, human level of existence.

Every society is basically a support group. People band together to set up an environment in which they can live peaceful, happy lives; an environment that helps them achieve the goals they want to achieve.

In order to do this, they come to an agreement about a way to live together. Most of what people in a society commit to one another is unwritten. It is just understood that people in a certain culture or civilization can be counted on to do some things and not to do other things.

In our society, for example, we expect that people will keep their clothes on in public, will not shoot each other on sight, will bathe often enough not to be offensive if they stand upwind, and will have just one husband or wife at a time. All this is part of our culture.

People in a society also accept laws, write constitutions, establish rules. In all of this they are making a covenant to help one another live according to some rational plan, according to principles they think will be beneficial to all.

Some laws people make for protection, to keep the environment free from influences that will destroy the things they love. Our society, for example, has laws to protect the ecology, to prevent the spread of disease, to ensure the security of private property.

Other laws give positive support to values people feel they need. Our society has passed laws to provide education, to encourage private businesses, to accelerate racial integration.

The laws of any society reflect its values, its priorities, its goals. In American society, for example, freedom of speech has a very high priority. Freedom from unsolicited sexual provocation does not. As a result, our news media cannot be controlled by politicians. A scandal such as Watergate cannot be hushed up by the guilty parties, and writers are free to express their own opinions in print.

But pornography can also be spread across every newsstand. Ordinary citizens driving down the street can be assailed by provocative pictures on billboards, and sex and violence run rampant on TV. No society is perfect.

The good laws in a country will help its citizens lead rational, healthy lives, not only physically but intellectually, emotionally and morally. Bad laws make it more difficult for people to think straight, to live by the values they believe in, or even to understand and embrace certain values in the first place.

By desegregating schools, for example, Americans reaffirmed their conviction that all people are created equal. Through civil rights laws people of both races have come to look on one another with less prejudice and more respect. These laws have corrected attitudes and taught values.

At the same time, by legalizing abortion, the American people denied the status of human life to infants just conceived. Human life inside the womb was declared unequal. Since that decision, the number of legal abortions per year in this country has jumped from an estimated 8,000 in 1967 to

1.3 million in 1977. People have abortions now who would never have dreamed of such a recourse 10 years ago. For millions of people, the abortion decision contributed to false attitudes and a distorted sense of values.

Clearly, the laws of a country have a lot to do not just with supporting attitudes and values but with determining them.

It isn't just laws, however, that determine a culture; it is how people act.

No man is an island. Everything people in a society do influences other people. And when a particular way of acting becomes widespread, then going against the trend can become as difficult as swimming against the tide.

Take the drug scene, for example. Up until the late 1940's, drug abuse was practically unknown in this country. Everyone had heard of marijuana, heroin and cocaine, of course, but they belonged to another world.

The reason for this was not just law, but the fact that people obeyed the law. People by and large agreed that such drugs were not good for the country. The result was that drugs just were not around. People were not offered the choice of experimenting with them. And most people, if you had asked them, would have said they did not want to be offered that choice. They had already chosen. They wanted drugs kept at a distance.

Then for all kind of reasons, more and more people began to break the drug laws. People did not sit down to discuss things rationally and to decide that it would be good to convert from a non-drug culture to a drug culture. No one ever argued, seriously at least, that pot among teenagers would be beneficial to them or to society. It just happened.

Once drugs were available, one individual after another succumbed to the temptation to use them. People gave in to the desire for a new experience, or to the urging of their friends, or to the compulsion to escape for a while from the reality of this world. And drug-abuse spread like wildfire.

It was abuse, not use. There was no calm, clear selection of goals and means, no rational program for improving society through drugs. Once the law against drugs was ignored—and it could not be enforced without the cooperation of the people—human passions took over. Civilization went out the window. The horse was loose and running, and no one was holding the reins.

Now it is no longer possible just to live peacefully and quietly without drugs. Young people who do not want to use them must positively resist both the pressures of the peer group and the urgings of their own curiosity or desire. Freedom from the immediate temptation of drugs is one of the freedoms our society no longer assures us, not because the laws have changed, but because people have changed.

All this adds up to saying that culture can both enlighten and confuse people. It can both liberate and enslave.

One particularly subtle kind of cultural enslavement results from advertising. It has turned manipulation into a science for the sake of making money.

Through ads, men are made to feel masculine

if they smoke the right kind of cigarette and drink the right brand of beer. The fear is planted that if they don't buy this kind of car, they will never have sitting next to them a girl as pretty as the one in the commercial. Ads suggest to women that if they don't look as sexy as a Hollywood star, can't get clothes white in the wash, can't brew a good cup of coffee, they are simply inadequate as women.

And so many people buy, not because they want something, but because they have been conditioned to think it will make them acceptable to other people. They buy, not because they want what they buy, but because they have been manipulated into feeling they have to have it.

We should not think that our decisions about sexual behavior are free from cultural conditioning and influences, either. No great new discovery launched the "sexual revolution" that characterizes our times. More people just started doing it and saying it was okay. Like drugs, sex just caught on. But once everyone is doing it—or everyone seems to be—it becomes hard for anyone not to.

No culture is totally good; no culture is totally bad. Seen as "civilization," society is a step up from savagery; it makes us more rational and free. Seen as "cultural conditioning," society can make us slaves. True freedom can never come from culture. And yet we can't find freedom without it.

The paradox of the human situation is that culture both broadens the horizon of our choices and narrows our choice down to one way of doing things.

As education, culture shows us options—new

attitudes and values—which we would never have discovered for ourselves. We learn that there is more than one way of doing things, more than one way of looking at reality and evaluating it. Culture gives us more to choose from.

At the same time, every given culture slants us toward one set of options. The same teacher or school that shows us alternative ways of looking at things prejudices us in favor of one particular way. This is almost inevitable.

Some people, when they recognize how enslaving culture can be, strike out for freedom by "dropping out" of their culture. They break with family and friends, school, religion and society. They sit in judgment on a world of which they are no longer a part. In order to be "free" they decide to listen to no one but themselves.

The problem with personalism

Many people struggling to escape the traps of cultural conditioning have adopted a philosophy of life called *personalism*—that is, they believe in nothing except what they are personally moved to do. At first glance, such a declaration of independence from culture seems like it would automatically make us free. And yet, left entirely to our own ideas and values, how narrow would we be?

Nothing is ultimately more enslaving than the worship of oneself. To make a cult of one's own ideas, of one's own attitudes and values; to follow nothing except what one can personally understand and appreciate—all of this comes dangerously close to making one's own self the ultimate criterion of truth and goodness, the final standard for judging

51

what is right and wrong.

And this is the definition of pride: to make oneself the criterion of truth and falsehood, of good and evil. Only God is that.

Besides, when we make a fetish out of being ourselves, we just wind up following spontaneous feelings and beliefs. Consciously or unconsciously, we make "doing what comes naturally" the norm for our behavior and for our ideals. And this leads us right back to where we began: to the primitive spontaneity of the infant or the savage.

We become the slaves of our psychological drives and hangups, of our own private allotment of emotions, desires and fears. We engage in sexual relations because they are "meaningful." We stop going to church because it isn't meaningful. We accept or do not accept other persons—other ideas, even—because they "turn us on" or "turn us off."

At best, to be left entirely to oneself is a stifling, suffocating kind of existence. People who aim at nothing higher than their own vision of truth, their own level of ideals wind up with a pretty low-ceiling life.

What is the answer to this? If we ourselves are not born with a total, intuitive grasp of all truth and goodness, then it would seem that the only way to be delivered from our own narrowness is to learn from somebody else. And that brings us back to culture again—but in a different way. We can choose carefully the guides from whom we will learn.

When we were children we put faith in our parents. That is how we grew and developed. We did things we did not understand until we came to understand them. We did things we had no particular desire to do—like going to school—until we decided from our own experience that these things were worthwhile.

Later we put faith in our culture. We took a lot of things for granted because the society we grew up in believed in them and recommended them to us. This is what it means to be a member of a culture—to put some faith in other people.

Even people who become disillusioned and "drop out" of their culture usually drop right into another culture—a sub-culture. They become revolutionaries, or hippies, or part of the drug scene. They join a cult or a commune.

They don't become free of culture; they just become part of the counterculture. They identify with another group, another philosophy of life, another style of living. And this is an act of faith—faith in the other people in the group; faith that through and with these others they will be able to arrive at a level of truth and happiness higher than what they had before or could achieve on their own.

To put faith in other people is not bad. It is *who* we put our faith in that makes the difference.

To be free is not to be uninfluenced. The totally uninfluenced person would have a mind like a blank wall, an emotional life as dead as the sands of the desert. To be free is to be influenced by those in whom we choose to put our faith.

And then we will be free only if they are worthy of our faith. If we put our faith in people who encourage us to be animals, we will lose our freedom to be human. If we put faith in those who encourage us to think and choose for ourselves, while at the same time presenting us with authentic truths to choose by, we will grow to deeper personal life.

But whom can we trust to do this? Any human being from whom we learn will to some extent impart personal prejudices, individual distortions of the truth. Any culture we belong to, no matter how good, is liable to enslave us.

How do we break out of the circle? What can we do to be free?

The only way out of the cycle, ultimately, is to share in the truth and the vision of God. It is only on the transcedent level of life that people can be totally free.

Freedom through transcendence

What Jesus offers is not just another cultural stance toward the world. He offers us a share in the vision of God himself. He offers us truths and values that come, not from any person or human society, but from God. He doesn't hesitate to say:

"If you live according to my teaching,
you are truly my disciples;
then you will know the truth,
and the truth will set you free."
(John 8:31-32)

Jesus doesn't call us out of culture entirely. We still remain citizens of this world. In fact, when God called his people—both in the Old Testament and in the New—he specifically called them into a culture: the culture of the Chosen People, the community of his Church. And in every age and place the word of God finds cultural expression—a variety of cultural expressions—in the language and customs of all the different peoples who believe.

But behind the variety of language and custom, behind the different forms of expression that Christians have given both to the word of God and to their response to it, stands the guiding person of Christ himself, still teacher, still head of his body, the Church. And what Jesus offers us as teacher are new options—options that lead to the fullness of life; options that come to us from the mind and heart of God himself.

If we follow those options—that is, if we make our choices according to his teaching—we will create ourselves according to the image of God. And this is to become what we were created to be. It is to enter the fullness of life.

In order to share in the life of God, we do have to break with our human culture in the sense of not letting it claim any priority of direction over our lives. God calls us out of our culture the way he called Abraham to leave his country, his kinsfolk and his father's house (Genesis 12:1); the way he called the Jews out of the slavery of Egypt (Exodus 3ff). God calls us to be "a chosen race. . .a holy nation, a people he claims for his own. . ." (1 Peter 2:9). This is why St. Paul exhorts us: "Prove yourselves innocent and straightforward, children of God beyond reproach in the midst of a twisted and depraved generation—among whom you shine like the stars in the sky while holding fast to the word of life" (Philippians 2:15-16a).

Christians expect to be different from the culture around them—not because they set out to be different, but because they set out to follow

Christ. His way is always different, his truth always more challenging than the way and the truth of this world.

To follow Christ is to be free: free from slavery to our physical appetites and desires; free from the human culture that enslaves us; free from the narrowness of our own limited personal vision and ideals.

Not that Christians—and the Christian community—don't ever make mistakes, or fail to appreciate the depth and the breadth of Christ's teaching. But the community and the culture to which the Christian relates is a community and culture guided by Christ, whose truth is beyond all culture, whose way leads to life in its fullness.

The freedom God offers us, then, is freedom through relationship with Christ his Son. To follow Christ is to break with our culture; not in the sense of dropping out, but in the sense of declaring ourselves emancipated from it, committed to another Way, another Truth, another Life.

5.

A Person Is a Chosen Stance
Our relationships create us

Once we realize what levels of life we have to work with, the next step in becoming a person is to enter into relationships. And this involves an exercise of choice.

It is our choices that create us as persons, our choices that give the meaning to our names.

A name is not the same as a definition. A definition answers the question, "What are you?" It tells what we are as *natures*. But a name answers the question, "Who are you?" It tells who we are as *persons*.

What our names mean to everyone who knows us, what they will mean when one day they are written on our tombstones, is nothing other than the sum total, the cumulative result, of all of our free responses to life. Who we are is something we are constantly creating by our responses to life.

In our society we may have lost sight of the deep significance of knowing someone's name. We call people by name—even by first name—whether we know them well or not. (I remember how surprised I was in France when I received a letter from a businessman signed with a deliberately unintelligible scrawl and underneath it only the typed word *Representative*. Here was a man who gave his title to his customers, and saved his name for his friends.)

In Scripture a tremendous importance is attached to knowing someone's name—and to the name itself. A name stands for a person. To reveal your name is to reveal your deepest self. To give someone a new name—for example, when God gave a new name to Abram in Genesis 17 and when Jesus gave a new name to Simon in Matthew 16—is to give a new mission and destiny in life.

When God sent Moses to the Israelites to lead them out of Egypt, Moses was afraid no one would believe that God had actually spoken to him. What he asked God to do, as a proof that he had entered into a special relationship with Moses, was to reveal his name:

> "But," said Moses to God, "when I go to the Israelites and say to them, 'The God of your fathers has sent me to you,' if they ask me, 'What is his name?' what am I to tell them?" God replied, "I am who am." Then he added, "This is what you shall tell the Israelites: I AM sent me to you. . . .
> "This is my name forever;

58

this is my title for all generations."
(Exodus 3:13-14, 15b)

God's name is the same from all eternity and for all ages, because God is already who he is. But our names are still in the process of acquiring the meaning they will have for all eternity because we are still creating ourselves as persons. We are "writing our names."

To the question "What is your name?" each of us could answer, "My name is 'Not-yet.' " Our names will not be fully written until our lives are finally lived.

The consequences of freedom

One of our first steps in becoming a person, then, is to realize that we are free, and that every free choice we make is an act of self-creation. What we do not only affects other people and things; every choice we make has an immediate effect on us as persons. It contributes to making us who we are.

If I choose to kick a cat, I have become related to that cat as kicker to kicked. The kick might make a lasting impression on the cat. But it has an even more lasting effect on me. My name now includes the relationship I have chosen to have with that cat: to kick it.

Freedom isn't just something nice to have, something that lets us do what we like without fear of consequences. There is no such thing as freedom without consequences.

With every free choice we make we are determining our being, shaping our personalities, giving an orientation to the direction of our lives, deciding what our names will mean forever. Anyone who chooses to do a loving thing, for example, is becoming a loving person. A person who tells a lie takes a step toward becoming a liar. We don't always like to look at our actions this way, but this is the truth of them nonetheless. All of our choices create us. Even the choice to kick a cat.

Choices are reversible, of course. The Prodigal Son who dropped out of his family in Chapter 15 of Luke's Gospel began with one relationship with his father. Then he chose to relate in a different way. And finally he came back and entered into a third relationship with his father that said more about him than either of the previous two.

All of our choices create us, but none creates us totally and irreversibly until we make our final choice at death. That is the significance of time for human beings. We are given time to create ourselves over and over until we get ourselves the way we want to be.

That is what life is. When we speak of our life on this planet we really mean our life-*time*—all the time that is ours between birth and death. Life is time for becoming.

The recognition of this truth—that time is for the sake of self-creation—led some of the Hindu wise men to the theory of reincarnation. They said that people just keep coming back to earth in one form after another until they finally get their being right. According to this hypothesis, life is like a school where no one can flunk out; you just keep repeating classes until you learn the lesson.

Many people are intrigued by the doctrine of reincarnation today. There is something comforting about it. It tells us that whatever we do, and however we use our freedom during this life, we cannot ultimately fail. Our bad choices cannot really create us as bad persons, because if they do we will just be sent back to start all over again until we get it right.

We may find comfort in the theory of reincarnation. But what this comfort really says of us is that, deep down, we are afraid of freedom. We do not want the responsibility of creating ourselves as persons. We are afraid we cannot handle it. We do not want our choices to count.

The flight from freedom

The acceptance of personal freedom, with all that it implies, is a profound and significant step along the way to becoming a person. It is not to be taken for granted. Psychologists spend hours helping people to uncover the little tricks and defense mechanisms they hide behind to avoid the responsibility of personal choice.

Husbands frequently won't sit down and talk to their wives. They use work as an excuse—"I just don't have the time, honey; I've got to get this done!"—because they are afraid of the choices they might have to face if they do.

Psychosomatic illness is another avoidance technique. Some people become invalids or have nervous breakdowns rather than confront the choices in their lives. Being sick is one way to get out of facing what you have to face. So people unconsciously make themselves sick rather than accept the responsibility of creating themselves as persons by the exercise of choice.

Rationalization is another defense against the consequences of freedom. Sometimes a girl on a date will suppress her own beliefs—her own convictions and ideals—rather than displease the boy she is dating. She does not say, "I'm doing something I don't believe in because he wants me to." She says, "I don't see anything wrong with what we are doing." But when she talks about it more deeply she admits that she does not feel comfortable with it.

Rationalization allows us to avoid making choices. It allows the girl on a date to keep up the illusion that she is being herself, that the other is respecting her as a person, and that everything she is doing is something she really believes in.

In reality she is conforming to what another person wants of her and letting herself be used rather than risk a breakup of the relationship. She is being a *what* instead of a *who* because freedom is too tough to handle.

Choosing relationships

Relationships are the key to being a person. They define us and give shape to our personalities the way boundaries give shape to a country or an outline to a silhouette. The shape of our personal existence, ultimately, is nothing but a profile of all the stances we have taken toward other persons and things, toward all the reality that is outside of us. *What* we are was determined by God; it was he who gave shape to our natures. But *who* we are is determined by us; and we can only give shape to our persons by deciding how we will relate to other beings.

62

The most important relationships for determining who we are are the relationships we have with other people. What is significant even in the way we relate to other things—to our possessions, for example, or to the ecology—is what it says about the way we relate to people.

Some friends encourage us to be ourselves. They challenge us to think deeply, to get in touch with our real ideals, to follow what we really believe in even if they would prefer us to act another way.

Other friends use us. They want us to do what pleases them, to conform to their attitudes and values, to their patterns of behavior and modes of self-expression. If we do, they reward us with love and support. If we do not, they make us feel isolated, guilty and alone. This can happen anywhere: in a family, a religion, a dating relationship, a cult.

When we choose to form a relationship with another person, it is important to ask how that other is going to relate to us. If the other is a user, we are going to be used. If the other is a manipulator, we are going to be manipulated. If the other's ideals are higher than our own, we are going to be helped to rise higher. If the other's ideals are lower than ours, then either we feel strong enough to pull the other up, or we should get ready to be pulled down.

Probably the best choices we have ever made, the most enlightened attitudes we have, our most beautiful ideals are somehow the result of interaction with other persons. It may have been a casual conversation, something we saw another do and were impressed by, a book we read (which is a real, if indirect, way of relating to the author), or the constant, mutual shaping of a longlasting friendship.

To choose a friend, then, is already in some degree to choose a pattern for our souls. Every friendship shapes us; and friends become like one another.

This is what makes the Incarnation of God in Jesus Christ so significant. In Jesus God drew near to us. He became a human being so that we could interact with him as human persons do with one another. He became available to us as a friend.

If we choose, we can let the person of Jesus Christ be the primary relationship in our lives. He will then be for us the friend whose words and example, whose constant interaction with us have the most influence over the choices we make, over the direction of our personal growth.

Relationship with Christ

People are afraid of freedom. They are afraid to take responsibility for their lives, for creating themselves as persons.

Many take refuge in defense mechanisms and self-deception—using any psychological contortion they can devise to avoid facing reality or responding to it with personal decision.

Others just refuse to grow up. Some remain on the feeling level all of their lives—"doing what comes naturally"—and refusing to think about the consequences. Some just follow the culture, letting it take them where it will. They find their security—and lose their identity—in being like everybody else.

Others abdicate their freedom to a group. The profusion of cults in our day points to how strong the temptation is just to turn one's freedom over to a charismatic leader or group and be carried through life like a baby in a womb.

Christ comes onto this scene offering two things: first, the security of God's own saving power and presence; but also a respect for human freedom so basic that no one can respond to Jesus Christ without at the same time discovering his or her own deepest self.

Therefore Jesus provides no psychological refuge. Of course he provides the security of a teacher, a guide, a companion, a friend who is the Incarnation of the saving power of God. But he does not relieve us of the necessity of choosing deeply and courageously for ourselves.

Jesus asked for absolute surrender of mind and will to himself—and then left this earth rather rapidly so that his followers could not turn over to him their responsibility for making the day-to-day decisions in their lives.

Anyone who follows Christ must put on the mind and heart of Jesus and no rules can take the place of personal judgment here. The decisions a person is called upon to make as a Christian in family life, social life, student or professional life are too varied, too multiple, too complex to be covered by any code of rules, no matter how exhausting. The teaching of Jesus contains very few rules if, in fact, it has any at all.

On the psychological level it is probably true to say that the heart and soul of so many cults or religions is security. This is the case with any approach to life that offers a fixed set of rules or the support of a totalitarian community as a substitute for continuing, personal choice.

The heart and soul of Christianity, on the other hand, is a chosen insecurity—the insecurity of those who are willing to risk everything in repeated personal decisions to follow the teaching of Jesus Christ in faith.

Christians are called to apply the teaching of Jesus to every decision and situation of life: at home, at school, on a date, on the job, in political options. They are asked to do this creatively, courageously, with personal understanding and insight. They must take the risk of deciding for themselves how the attitudes and values of Christ would require them to act in every given set of circumstances. And they need the courage to live out their ideal no matter how much it costs them, no matter how much conflict it causes in themselves, with their peer group or their culture. Only someone who is willing to take up the responsibility of being a person can accept this insecurity.

The Christian community can help. Through the Church we learn the teachings of Jesus and get our first formation in how to apply them to life. The community will help us with some rules—the Ten Commandments (which came through Moses not through Jesus Christ), and with whatever other rules the Church makes in any given moment of history as a communal response to the challenges and problems of the times.

But the Church will not accept being made a substitute for personal decision and choice. The Church is a community of sure doctrine and clear moral values. But it is also a community that challenges the individual to make deep, personal decisions.

In Jesus then, and in his body on earth, the Church, we have an answer to the human fear of responsibility. Jesus does not relieve us of the responsibility for making choices; he just gives us the courage to make them. He does not provide the psychological support of a community which does our thinking for us. But he does promise the support of the invisible—and incomprehensible—power and direction of God.

That is the significance of the Incarnation of Christ: It makes possible a relationship with God through which we can discover and create ourselves in response to the mind and heart of God.

Three steps to personhood

Becoming a person, then, involves three things:

1) *Accepting the fact that we have the power of choice.* There are options in life. Each of us can—and eventually must—decide what our goals in life will be, and what means will be most effective in bringing us to our goals. To let other people (the culture, our peer group) determine the direction of our lives is to choose not to be a person, not to have a name.

2) *Realizing that every free choice creates us as persons.* We are the sum total of our choices. That is what our names mean now, and what they will mean when they are finally written on our tombstones. Every free choice is a word of self-creation.

3) *Choosing our relationships.* Every free choice is a response to some reality outside of ourselves. When we decide how we will interact with and relate to other persons and things—and to God—we are deciding who we will be as persons. We are writing our names.

No one can create himself or herself alone. Each of us becomes a person through interacting with other people and with God. With whom we choose to interact and how—whether as a *what* or as a *who;* whether deeply or superficially; whether to be manipulated or molded by others or to create ourselves by responding to each as free persons: these are the choices that will make us who we are.

6.

The 'Master of the Way'
Creating ourselves through discipleship

The first Christians called Jesus the "Master of the Way."

His religion was not called a "religion" then; it was just "this new way"—the new way of living that Jesus taught. (See Acts of the Apostles 18:25-26; 19:9, 23). And Jesus was a "master" of the way to live, a teacher whose own way of living was so inspiring that people wanted him to teach them how to follow it.

One of the first things the Gospels tell us about Jesus is that "the people were spellbound by his teaching because he taught with authority, and not like the scribes" (Mark 1:22). Jesus taught as one who knew. And he knew because he lived, and lived perfectly, everything he taught.

There is an old Chinese proverb which sums

71

up the stages of human wisdom thus:

I hear, and I forget;
I see, and I understand;
I do—and I know.

Many of those who heard the words of Jesus went off and forgot what he said. But those who saw his actions understood. And those who began to *live* by what he taught came to know for themselves his truth.

The same pattern is true today. Jesus is a teacher. If we want to, we can learn from him and he will teach us everything he knows.

But first we have to relate to him as a person.

To be a teacher in the time of Christ—especially a teacher of how to live—meant a lot more than just standing up in front of a random gathering of people and explaining to them something they didn't know.

A teacher was someone who entered into a deep, personal relationship with those he accepted to teach. They were more than just students in the sense that the word has for us today. They were *disciples*. When the teacher accepted them as his disciples, he agreed to form their lives, to give his own shape to their hearts and minds.

And the disciples accepted this from him. They were people who related as much to the person of the teacher as to his words. They modeled their lives on him—not just on what he said, but on what he did.

In order even to be a disciple in Jesus' time, you had to be committed. A disciple could not be a detached listener sitting in a classroom, taking away only what had appeal. A disciple was committed to learning, to embracing, to putting into practice everything the teacher taught.

Obviously, no one became the disciple of another without a lot of heavy thought. It was a serious act of decision. It involved a lot of faith in the person of the teacher.

The same is true today for those who would be disciples of Jesus Christ. To learn from him— even to be taught by him—we have to be committed in advance.

This means that the first question is not what Jesus says to us, but who he *is* for us. To decide this, we must listen to his words and look at what he did. But before his words can really teach us, we must come to a decision about the man who spoke them.

Searching for sages

A few years ago *Newsweek* guest columnist Joyce Maynard, 19, spoke for the young people of her generation:

"We're all in search of sages," Maynard wrote ("Searching for Sages," Dec. 25, 1972*). But our society doesn't seem to believe in any.

And so, she continued, "Just about every suburban-born, college-bred boy I know has a hitch-hiking story about 'this real great truck driver' he met. . .who. . .'knows what it's all about.' He's usually called Joe or Red. . . . He is a philosopher of the road who has given the boy. . .some parting nuggets of Truth as he lets him out at Exit 1 for New Haven or Exit 23 for Cambridge, some

---

words of wisdom the boy now imparts to me over coffee and. . .cigarettes in the campus grill."

It is the absence of true sages—men and women of deep sensibility—that leads us, according to Maynard, to make false gods of rock poets and B-grade philosophers. "We," she says, "who so hated school, are now in search of *teachers.* An apricot-robed, lotus-folded guru with a name too long to fit on one line of a poster, an old man on a park bench (with a beard if possible), a plain-talking, no-nonsense Maine farmer. . . , the author of any slim volume of austere prose or poetry. . .—we attend their words so abjectly, sometimes even literally sit at their feet, waiting for any crumb of what will pass as wisdom to be offered us."

Maynard's answer is Jesus—not the Jesus of her childhood religion, necessarily, but Jesus, the "Master of the Way."

"Jesus has come out of the closet," she says. "The disenchanted and the ones never enchanted in the first place are returning to the fold with a passion. . . . It is a sign of many things. . . . What's really going on, though. . .is our search for a prophet, for someone who can, for a change, tell us the answers. (The big line I remember from our school days was 'There is no one right answer. What's your *opinion?*' "

And her conclusion is: "After so many unprofound facts and so much loose, undisciplined freedom, it's comforting to have a creed to follow and a cross to bear."

We have already seen that the teaching of Jesus is a comfort only if we have the courage to shoulder the responsibility for making personal

decisions about our lives. The answers of Jesus—
and he gives them—are sure and challenging guidelines. They don't relieve us of the insecurity of personal decision and choice; but they do constitute,
as his first listeners exclaimed about him, "a completely new teaching in a spirit of authority"
(Mark 1:27).

The teaching of Jesus did not end with his
death and resurrection. For most of those who
came to believe in him, that is when it really began.

After he had risen from the dead and
ascended into heaven, Jesus sent his Spirit into the
hearts of his apostles. From that moment on he
continued to teach through his Church, as he still
does today.

People gathered to hear his words proclaimed
by the apostles, to ask an explanation of what they
meant, to discuss together how to apply them to
the concrete reality of their own lives. They believed, as we still believe, that Jesus was present
and speaking to them personally—through his
Word, through his Church, through his Spirit dwelling in their hearts. They believed in him as a teacher risen and living, still present, still forming them
as Master of the Way.

They believed he had answers people could
live by; a doctrine about life that cast light on the
choices people have to make every day—choices in
their social life, their family life, their student or
professional life, their civic life. They believed that
Jesus could lead them to the fullness of life. And,
more than this, they believed that he could give
them a way of sharing in the life of God through
the outpouring of his Spirit.

Their first step was to study his Word.

Jesus taught through words

Every teaching involves not just content, but
method. For understanding what a teaching says
about human life, one is as important as the other.

Jesus did not begin as teacher by proposing to
his followers a method of meditation or a system
of ascetical practices. He did not tell them how to
sit or how to stand, what to eat or what to wear.
He did not hold out to them a series of exercises
that would lift them to a higher state of consciousness.

He just began to talk.

He talked about attitudes and values, moral
choices. He talked about the way people should
speak to one another, think about one another, act
toward one another. He talked about the attitude
we should take toward God, about God's attitude
toward us.

He taught us a simple formula of petitions to
address to God. The Lord's Prayer, or "Our Father," was probably meant to give us a list of priorities to guide our petitions to God rather than a
fixed formula of words to recite. In order to teach
us how to pray, Jesus first taught us what to pray
for.

The method of Jesus as teacher was to work
through the human intellect and heart to call for
an exercise of free choice. In Jesus God came to us
as a human being. He taught as a human being. His
teaching was pitched to the human level of understanding and appreciation.

He called us to rise higher than the human.

But he taught us to rise by first using the natural powers God gave us: the power to think and to choose.

I once wrote a book called *His Way*, (St. Anthony Messenger Press, 1977). It contains a method for meditating on the Scriptures, for reflecting on the words of Christ. A college student who read the book wrote me that the best thing she got out of the book was the freedom to *think* about what Jesus said:

> I learned, most importantly, to listen.
> I heard many times that God speaks through Scripture, but it never really sunk in. I used to get so frustrated and angry at myself because I thought the way to listen was to quiet your mind and just sort of "tune in." I have never been able to quiet my mind. It's been forever babbling on, questioning and answering and wandering. I don't know where I got the idea, but it sure is difficult (for me, next to impossible) to empty one's head to become a receiver for heavenly tidings. I guess that's a prayer for the "graduated." But for beginners it's murder!
>
> Now, sometimes I find a phrase, or even the way a word is used, and the different meanings it may have, and I work on it — sort of chew on it for awhile. And when I realized that what I was mulling over applied to a few questions I had been carrying, I could have been knocked over by a feather. *It's tremendous!*

There is nothing unchristian about "emptying the head" for prayer. A whole Christian mystical tradition is built on such a method, in fact. The point is that Jesus did not start people with that.

He started them off being human—thinking about the words of God and responding to them the way people think about and respond to anyone else's words.

He came to us as a human being, and all he asks—in the beginning, at least—is that we respond to him as human beings, using the equipment God gave us to work with.

I have met many people who said, "I don't know how to pray." I have never met anyone who said, "I don't know how to think." Praying over the Scripture is nothing other than thinking about the words and actions of Jesus until you come to some decisions that affect the way you live.

The key word here is *until*.

The difference between praying over the Scriptures and just reading them for entertainment, or with intellectual curiosity, is all in the word *until*. The disciple reads the words of Jesus with the intention of reflecting on them *until* he or she comes to *decisions*.

Jesus said his words were like seeds cast into the ground: The fruit they bear depends on how they are received. Alone, the words of Jesus do not change anyone's life. Decisions in response to the words of Jesus will change everyone's life.

Jesus is not real to us until we begin to take him for real. Until his reality has some influence on our lives we do not really know he is there.

The first act of discipleship, then, is to confront the words of Jesus Christ in Scripture; to take them seriously, reflect on their meaning and application to our lives, and make decisions based on them.

>We hear, and we forget;
>We see, and we understand;
>We do—and we *know*!

In Jesus Christ God became man so that we could interact with him in a human way. Because Jesus is God-made-man we can have with God, through Jesus Christ, a relationship of personal knowledge and love, of discipleship and formative friendship that lets us create ourselves as persons through interaction with the personality of God himself.

Jesus came to lead us to the highest level of sharing in the life of God. But he begins by teaching us, in a very human way, just how to think and make choices in response to his words.

And this is how our following of him begins.

7.

Being A Word Made Flesh

Expressing our relationship with Christ

Jesus is the answer to the *why* of human living.

Why did God make us? For relationship with himself.

Why do we exist? Why are we alive? To enter into relationship with Jesus Christ, and through him into relationship with God.

If we become disciples of Jesus, we are recognizing the basic *why* of our existence. But where do we go from there? Where does discipleship lead us?

We are called, as disciples of Jesus, not just to learn from him, but to express what we learn. Those who come to Jesus as disciples he sends out again as witnesses and apostles.

There are no simple "followers" of Jesus.

Everyone who follows him must learn to *lead*.

Through his teaching and example Jesus offered new options to mankind, options that transform entirely one's way of relating to other people, to work, to family, to life and to death:

• "Love your enemies" (Matthew 5:44).

• "When someone slaps you on one cheek, turn and give him the other; when someone takes your coat, let him have your shirt as well" (Luke 6:29).

• "Do not worry about your livelihood, what you are to eat or drink or use for clothing" (Matthew 6:25).

• "Do not fear those who deprive the body of life. . .do not be afraid of anything" (Matthew 10:28, 31).

• "He who seeks only himself brings himself to ruin, whereas he who brings himself to nought for me discovers who he is" (Matthew 10:39).

These are inspiring words; words of hope and challenge. The words of Jesus, however, cannot bear fruit on earth unless they are embodied in action.

The world only listened to Jesus, only took him seriously, because he lived what he preached. The Good News was not in what he said, but in what he did. Words are never news; only actions are.

For a person to say he is a Christian or a disciple of Jesus Christ hardly has meaning anymore. Words are too easy; it doesn't cost anything to say we believe.

Not only in the eyes of God, but also in the eyes of the world our words have only the value of our actions. That is why no one can be a witness to

Jesus Christ, or proclaim the Good News of Christ in the world, unless he gives his body to give flesh to Jesus' words. We must answer the call of Christ with flesh and blood, not air.

In Jesus Christ the Word of God took flesh. That is what made God's love real to us. In our lives the words of Jesus must take flesh or his reality will be lost to the world.

And so the real *why* of our existence is not just to be disciples of Jesus Christ, to learn from him, to enter into relationship with his mind and will and heart. The real *why* of our existence on earth is to be the body of Christ.

If this sounds like something of a mystery, that's because it is. But we have not understood the full "breadth and length and height and depth" of the life that is offered to us on earth unless we understand that what we are really called to do is to give our bodies to be the body of Christ.

We are called to let Christ live again in us, so that we might live in him the life that is proper to God—and live it here on earth.

St. Paul put it all in two sentences: "And now, brothers, I beg you through the mercy of God to offer your bodies as a living sacrifice holy and acceptable to God, your spiritual worship. Do not conform yourselves to this age but be transformed by the renewal of your mind, so that you may judge what is God's will, what is good, pleasing and perfect" (Romans 12:1-2).

"Offer your bodies as a living sacrifice"

What God asks us to do is offer our bodies, give him our flesh and blood while we are here on

82

earth. Jesus needs bodies to live and work for him on earth, living people to cooperate with him in the work of bringing his Good News to the whole human race and letting it transform every human activity.

It is live bodies Jesus needs, not dead ones. We are not talking here about human sacrifice, much less about robots or zombies who move only as they are directed to move, with no minds or wills of their own.

The bodies Jesus calls for are bodies with intellects and wills, whole human persons. He asks us to put ourselves and all of our human powers at his disposition so that he might live and act in us. He does not wish to suppress what is human within us or leave it aside, but by enlisting it in his service, to lift it up to the level of his own life. He wants to act in and through our human thoughts, desires and choices with his own light and life and love.

He asks us to live; but to live in such a way that it is no longer just we who live, but Christ who lives in us (see Galatians 2:20).

This means that in all the places where we really live our lives—at home, at school, on dates, at parties and at work—we are there as "living sacrifices," our bodies offered to God to express the truth, the love, the values of Jesus Christ in everything we do.

In our social life, our family life, our school life and at work, we are called to have no other goal except to do what we are doing in a way that gives glory to God; that is, in a way that lets the power and triumph of Christ's death and resurrection, the reality of his grace and presence, the beauty of his truth and love appear in human flesh again.

This is what it means to offer our bodies as a living sacrifice, to God, to be the body of Christ.

"Do not conform yourselves to this age"

We cannot do this, however, if our loyalty is divided.

In order to be given to Christ we must declare ourselves emancipated from our culture. We must give up the desire to fit in and not count on being accepted. We must be willing to break with the attitudes and values of our peer group, to think and act in a way that is different, and to suffer any kind of retaliation our society imposes on those who do not conform.

The young sometimes think that adults are conformists, while they, the young, are not. The truth is, the young conform as much to the manners and morals, the language, dress, behavior and thought patterns of their own age group as adults do to theirs—if not more so.

This stands to reason. The young are often less secure. They are still looking for their identity, still trying to establish their self-worth. They may accept with their heads what we said in an earlier chapter about the value of a person depending only on his or her choices; but in their hearts they are not sure. They need the affirmation of friends, the acceptance of their peer group. They find it very difficult to be alone.

It takes courage to walk not really alone, but with Christ instead of with the visible support of a crowd. Until we muster that courage our loyalty is divided; we are trying at one and the same time to follow Christ and the culture.

This is not to say that the culture is all bad, or that we as Christians must set out in principle to be different in every way from everyone around us. Much, probably most, of our culture is good. As one of the young people who read the manuscript of this book put it, "My own small world is surrounded as much with love and goodness as with evil—more!"

It is not a matter of condemning the culture, but of being free in our relationship to it. St. Paul, in telling us not to conform, simply means that to be given to Christ we must put our loyalty to him ahead of all the attitudes and values of our culture, ahead of all its movements and trends, ahead of all the acceptance any other person or group can offer us.

We must decide what our priorities are. If we want to be given to Christ we must make his values, his principles and ideals more important to us than what other people are doing, wearing, driving, drinking, smoking, striving for in life or saying about us. We have to have the courage to be guided from within, not from without.

This is a prerequisite for love. We must possess ourselves before we can give ourselves away.

"But be transformed by the renewal of your mind"

We don't break with the culture simply to be psychologically free to receive the teachings of Jesus with an open mind.

What Jesus promises us is not simply information, but transformation. He doesn't just give us a new set of principles and values to work with; he lifts us up to the level of his own thinking and choosing. He gives us the power to see and judge things in a different way, his own way, God's way.

When we give our bodies to him, he sends his Holy Spirit to live and act in us, to know and love within our very hearts. He gives us his Spirit so that by participating in his own activity within us we might see what he sees, love what he loves, and personally choose with the vision and the vigor of God himself.

This is what it means to "be transformed by the renewal of your mind." It is the fulfillment of the promise God made through his prophet Jeremiah long ago: "I will place my law within them, and write it upon their hearts" (Jeremiah 31:33). We become enlightened from within. Where no fixed laws or rules can tell us what to do, we see and judge by the light of the one who makes all laws with the vision of God himself.

The light that enlightens us is the very presence and power of God dwelling within us. If we offer our bodies as a living sacrifice to him, he gives his whole self to us. And this is eternal life.

"So that you may judge . . ."

The effect of this transformation of our minds is that we become able to judge not only what is good as opposed to evil, but also what is pleasing to God—the better thing to do—and even what is perfect, what Jesus himself would do in our situation.

This is the meaning of the text of St. Paul

that we have cited. All this is implied in the invitation to "offer our bodies as a living sacrifice to God."

This is the true *why* of our existence.

In the pages that follow we are going to talk about an ideal of sexual morality that is far from being "conformed to the spirit of this age." Those who are able to accept it—and even to rejoice in it—will choose to "be transformed by the renewal of their minds" and to "offer their bodies as a living sacrifice to God."

This is an ideal that goes beyond people's natural understanding of themselves. It is an ideal based on the *what* and *who* and *why* of human life as seen in the life of Jesus.

That is why it is important to ask ourselves, "Who is the person of Jesus Christ for me?" and "What do I choose to be for him?"

Is he the Master of the Way for me? Do I place my trust in him deliberately and wholeheartedly and choose him to be the teacher and friend who will form my life?

Am I committed to living by his words, no matter where they lead? Am I ready to be his disciple without any reservations?

The challenge of living as the body of Christ in everything we do can be enormous. It can seem overwhelming at times. Yet this is the *why*—and the glory—of our existence.

Part II:
The Good News
About Sex

The good news about people is that we are called to the fullness of life. We are called to this through relationship with Jesus Christ. We are called to live simultaneously on four levels: the physical, the cultural, the personal and the transcendent, which means "spiritual" or "graced."

The good news about sex is that it has meaning and value on all four of these levels:

• As a physical reality, sex is delightful, lifegiving and human.

• As a cultural reality, sex is enriching and challenging.

• As a personal reality, sex creates us as loving persons; it brings our love to life and makes us one with each other.

• As a graced reality, sex is God expressing himself through us.

89

In the chapters which follow, we will explore the meaning and value of sex on each of these levels. We begin with the physical reality of sexual intercourse as an expression of our humanity.

8.

Pleasure, Purpose and Humanity

Sex as a human act

Does sex have value?

All of us would probably agree it does, but why? What, precisely, is the value of sex?

"It's fun!"

"Sex gives life; you have babies."

"It's the expression of love. It helps you get closer together."

These are the answers I have received most often in discussing the value of sexual relations with the young.

Let's begin with the most basic value, one which every person and society recognizes, even if we don't always consciously make the connection: Sex is for the sake of having children.

We are not saying that sex is only for the sake of having children, or that two people can never have sex together for any other reason. We are just recognizing the obvious: The reason why human beings, like other mammals, come in two varieties—male and female—is in order to reproduce.

Some people would take issue with the words, "in order to." "Human beings are not male and female," they would argue, "*in order to* reproduce. They just happen to be male and female; and as a consequence they *can* reproduce."

To say this is to reject—on the level of sexuality, at least—one of the basic arguments for the existence of God: the argument from design. And since it helps in understanding ourselves—and our sexuality—to know whether we were designed to be this way, or whether we just happened to evolve this way (*by chance*, that is, since evolution can also be by design) it might be worth going off on a tangent for a few minutes just to say a word about this question.

Sex—by chance or by design

The real point at issue here is not the question of God's existence. It is the question of human rationality: Are we really able to think?

Can we read a book with a plot as complex as that of *A Tale of Two Cities*, for example, and not really know that another human person wrote that book?

Or is it possible for our minds to accept that the book could have been produced by chance, over millions of years, by a multitude of monkeys playing in a print shop?

Physically, the monkeys could have punched all the right keys. But there is no way we can believe that the story in that book could be there unless a human mind meant to tell it.

Computers do marvellous things today. They seem almost able to reason. But in reality computers cannot do anything they are not programmed to do by a human brain.

Whoever—or whatever—produced the human brain has to be at least as intelligent as the brain that designed the computer.

It is quite possible that the human body evolved from lower forms of life—evolved, that is, to such a point that it was able to house a rational soul created by God. But if it did evolve, it was programmed to evolve.

No more comes out of a process than what went into it. If the end result is something we can recognize as intelligible, rational, understandable, then some intelligent, rational being who understood what he was doing had something to do with the program.

If we ever get a letter from outer space, we won't have any doubt someone wrote it—someone we can communicate with on a rational, intellectual level.

But almost everything in nature is a letter to us from God.

To go back to our first example: If we ever find ourselves able to believe that a book like *A Tale of Two Cities* was typed out by chance, then what we are really doing when we deny a human author is denying that the book is a story in the first place.

If the book was typed haphazardly by monkeys, then it was never intended to tell a story.

There is no real plot. No word in it was meant to be a word. There is nothing between the covers of the book but some ink smudges that happened to occur in that order.

If we read some of those ink smudges as letters and as words, we are deceiving ourselves. We are reading into the ink blots on the page a meaning they were never intended to have—a meaning they do not have.

In other words, the day we deny that anybody meant the book to say what it says to us, we have denied our own capacity to recognize meaning and intelligibility in reality. We are denying our own ability to tell the difference between a book someone wrote and a bunch of ink blots on a page. This is like saying we aren't really sure there's any difference between the Rocky Mountains and the New York skyline. The buildings in New York look like they might have been built by human hands. But you never can be sure—maybe they were caused by an earthquake.

The same thing is true of the sexual differences between men and women.

If we ever get to the point where we really think a woman's breasts just happened to grow that way—and that then a woman just happened to find that they could be used to nourish a baby, we are in bad shape. There is a connection between breasts and babies—not a connection we read into reality, but a relationship we find there.

Anyone, therefore, who accepts the human intellect as a valid, rational power can see that human sexuality is designed for procreation.

Suppose that women existed but men didn't—

or vice versa. The sexual organs of either one would be pure nonsense, totally unintelligible, without any reason for existing. They would be like parts on a machine that had no function at all, and no purpose whatsoever for being there. We would have to look at the human body and conclude that it just did not make sense.

Or suppose that a woman had ovaries but no womb; or a womb, but no breasts; or breasts without hormones to trigger the production of milk. Each individual organ is totally purposeless without the others.

There is no explanation for the way humans are built unless somebody planned us this way. We don't know how many years it took for the human body to evolve, or by what precise process God made it evolve. But we do know that its evolution was programmed and the final result was planned.

Consider the time factor.

The whole complicated system of sexual anatomy had to evolve at the same time, in the same place, and in men and women simultaneously. If it had not, if just one of the organs had been missing in the first bodies to evolve (or if males had evolved at a different time and place from females), reproduction could never have taken place. The first human beings to evolve would have died without progeny. Then the whole evolutionary process would have had to start all over again from scratch.

If sex was designed in us by the Creator who designed and planned the rest of our human nature, then we have to respect the purposes behind his design.

Two obvious facts strike us at once:

First, the sexual organs of men and women were designed in view of each other. *Sex is something meant to happen between males and females.*

Second, the sexual organs are obviously designed for reproduction. *Sex is meant to be connected with the giving of new life.*

Sex—for the sake of new life

The first, most basic value of sex, then, is that through sexual relations between men and women new life is brought into the world. Only those who have had the experience of actually giving life can appreciate how much this really means.

No culture has ever denied the connection between sexuality and the value of giving life. But many cultures, and ours is one of them, can obscure this connection to the point of almost forgetting—and causing others to forget—that it is there.

Many persons and elements active in our culture today teach us beautiful attitudes toward sex: attitudes of meaning and commitment, of respect for our own and others' integrity as human persons. Other elements in our culture, however, are not so helpful. These do not deny the true meaning of sex so much as they ignore it. What this side of our culture produces in us is not so much false theories about sex as false *associations*.

Just one small example: Ours is a very breast-conscious culture. The clothes styles, the calendar pin-ups, the topless bars, even the omnipresent brassiere ads combine to keep us so. But western culture—in contrast to countries like India, Africa and Japan—conditions us to associate the female breast only with sexual arousal, not with mother-

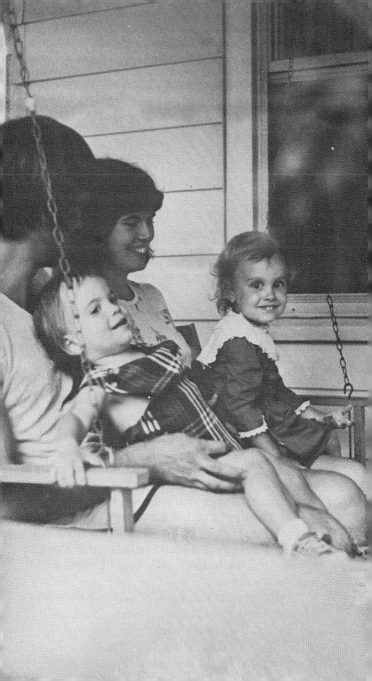

hood and the nurturing of children.

Our concept of modesty allows clothes that give prominence to sexual characteristics in a way physically provocative to men, but discourages nakedness that would be natural or healthy. For example, women are invited to present their breasts almost completely uncovered as sex symbols in public, but custom requires them to nurse their babies in private.

As a result we grow up seeing breasts in every context except that of the beautiful purpose to which they were designed.

This conditions men to see women not as friends or persons, or potential wives and mothers, but as sex objects. It is as objects of sexual desire—not as bearers of the true value and dignity of sex—that our society makes women most visible.

In the measure that we are influenced by the sexually exploitative side of our culture, we associate sex with pleasure but not with purpose. We associate sexual intercourse with intense physical and psychological enjoyment but not with the giving of new life. We associate sexual experiences with the youthful romanticism of dating, and not with the mature love of marriage. We teach girls to associate femininity with sexual attractiveness, not with potential motherhood—or the personal complementarity of the sexes. And if the pleasure-oriented elements of our society fail, by and large, in teaching males to be good lovers, they hardly even hint at the connection between maleness, or virility, and the lasting, daily task of being a husband and father.

All the associations our culture makes for us

between sex, pleasure and passion are real, of course, except for some obvious distortions. It is not the associations we make that are so misleading; it is the associations we do not make.

If we associate sex with pleasure, that is truth. If we do not associate sex with parenthood, that is a mistake.

When I was in high school we were given an explanation of sexual morality that fell somewhat short of the truth. Everything we were told was true; it was even helpful. I make use of it in teaching today. It just didn't give the whole picture.

Since then I have learned a lot of what we were not taught. I learned it with the help of our culture—and especially of the young who were struggling with the problem of how to reconcile the good values which our culture is conscious of today with certain ways of acting that are not so good, but which the culture seems almost to impose.

In later chapters I would like to share the most recent values I have learned. But here I want to begin with the first one—and with a very basic guideline that follows from it. This guideline is incomplete in itself, but it is true. And it can be extraordinarily helpful: *Sex is for the sake of having children.*

The argument that follows from this can be put in a very negative form, and to some extent it was put that way to my generation. According to the argument we got, what God really wanted from sex was children. This is why he made people male and female. Children, however, cannot just be mass-produced. They have to be raised and cared for individually, one-by-one. Children need families to grow up in.

But, it was pointed out to us, many people—especially males, perhaps—would shy away from the responsibilities and burdens of family life. After all, once you get into it, supporting and raising children can become a 24-hour-a-day job.

So God gave people a strong physical appetite, the appetite for sex. It was just a fact, like the appetite for food. And he made a rule: Anybody who wants to satisfy this appetite must do so inside marriage, nowhere else.

Sex was the bait. Marriage was the trap. Inside marriage you could have all the sex you wanted. Outside marriage, no touching, no tasting.

This was a pretty clear rule. And it worked—especially when you told anyone who went against it that he or she was heading straight for hell!

Our judgment of what does and does not constitute subjective moral guilt is a little more nuanced today. We are no longer so quick to say a person is—or is not—on the path to eternal rejection of God. But this rule, just as a guideline for behavior, is still a true and valid rule. I would defend it today. Sexual pleasure is for the married. They are the only ones who have the right to the enjoyment of sex as such, although there are many things we might tend to identify as sexual pleasure which are not really sexual at all. (We will speak of these later, in Part III).

The trouble is, the explanation behind the rule didn't seem to place much value in sexual relations themselves. If sex was just a bait, then it was hardly anything very noble in itself. The pleasure of sexual intercourse was just something God invented to get people to procreate. The real value of sex seemed not to be in the act of sex itself, but in what resulted from it: babies.

Having babies was the value. Sex came across as just a means to an end. Small wonder that some people grew up to consider the means disgusting. St. Augustine, for example, explained that the holy men of the Old Testament would not have sought intercourse if they could have had children in any other way! England's Queen Victoria is said to have described her acceptance of intercourse with these words: "I just close my eyes and think of England!"

More than bait for babies

The idea that God would simply bait us into action is something we find degrading—especially if the action is as deep and as personal as sex.

And yet, seeing purpose and design in sex does give it value.

What made sex rational and human—and ultimately dignifying—to people of old was the fact that sex had a purpose they could understand and identify with, a purpose they could make their own. It was not blind animal instinct. They saw the act of intercourse as an act of cooperating with God; a chosen, responsible decision to continue the human race.

And they were right—not in seeing procreation as the only value in sex, but in seeing that sex for pleasure alone makes an animal of a person.

Two people can engage in sexual relations with no other conscious thought than to give pleasure to one another. This is not only good psychology at times; it is also good theology. Sex should be fun.

But if this pleasure-giving does not occur in a context of committed personal love; if the two people involved don't understand sex as more than a mutual excitation, then the stimulation they provide each other's bodies will act as a depressant on the soul. As persons it will tear them down.

A whole school of thought in our day would have us see sex not as more than just pleasure for the sake of procreation, but as less than that: pleasure for the sake of pleasure, *period.*

One spokesman for this school of thought is *Playboy*. In the *Playboy* philosophy—designed and written for men—sex is just for playing, and women are nothing but playmates. Any involvement with the female with whom you choose to play beyond the exploitation of the present moment is an unenlightened mistake.

To build any sexual relationship on this philosophy is to deal in pure fiction. Real men and women cannot be reduced to nothing but friendly partners in pleasure. Harvey Cox points out in *The Secular City* (Macmillan, 1966): "Much as the human male might like to terminate his relationship with a woman as he would snap off the stereo, or store her for special purposes like a camel's hair jacket, it really can't be done. And anyone with a modicum of experience with women knows it can be done. Perhaps this is the reason *Playboy 's* readership drops off so sharply after the age of 30."

It is easy for us to be critical of people like St. Augustine, for whom sex was saved from animality only through the human ability to relate it consciously to the value of giving life. But when we remember that the young Augustine came out of a civilization which had already sunk to *Playboy's* level, his reactions are more understandable. By his own admission, Augustine at 16 could not tell the difference between love and lust. When he was engaged to be married, and accordingly got rid of his mistress, he found himself unable to do without sex until the wedding. So he took another woman to sleep with while he was waiting!

And yet this same Augustine, when his first mistress bore him a child outside of marriage, had the depth of understanding and appreciation to name the boy Adeodatus—the Latin for "given-by-God." (See *The Confessions* of St. Augustine, Book 2, Chapter 2; and Book 3, Chapter 15.)

There are many good things about our culture, though there is hardly anything that cannot be improved. But one area which is in sore and urgent need for improvement right away is our respect for human sexuality and life. They go together.

In practice, however, respect for either one is all but impossible if we continue to dissociate the pleasure of sexual relations from the privilege of giving life. Yet this disassociation has to be made by those who seek to justify sexual relations outside of marriage.

Fear of pregnancy

For those who are not married, sexual intercourse by its very nature carries with it a fear of pregnancy—or it should!

According to a 1974 report of the Department of Health, Education and Welfare, three out of 10 teenage girls who have sex outside of marriage bear a child out of wedlock. That is almost 33 1/3 percent. Statistically, a girl has a little less chance of avoiding pregnancy in premarital sex than she does of avoiding rape or violence if she hitchhikes. (About 25 percent of girls who hitchhike are assaulted.)

The pill has not helped very much, nor any other methods of contraception. Not only do they not always work, but teenagers generally do not use them. A girl is not likely to be taking the pill or her date to be carrying contraceptives unless the two of them have decided, with conscious deliberation and planning, to go out and have intercourse together. It usually doesn't happen that way.

Probably no nation in the history of the world has been more conscious than ours of contraception, or more technically skilled in its methods. In spite of this, the number of illegitimate births among teenagers doubled between 1940 and 1961. And now every year approximately one million girls between the ages of 15 and 19 become pregnant.

Of this number, some 150,000 miscarry. Another 250,000 have abortions. The babies born to the remaining 600,000 make up one fifth of all the babies born in the United States each year.

These are just physical realities. They mean that every couple who engage in intercourse outside of marriage deeply know, even in the midst of their sexual act, that the chances are roughly one out of three they will have to make a decision to marry because of a pregnancy, to keep the baby and raise it without being married, to give the child up for adoption or to have an abortion.

Whether we consciously think about this decision or not, it is there. And it is there in our subconscious even while the act of intercourse is going on. We would be naive to think that this knowledge does not affect the experience.

Any experience of sexual relations that is at the same time an experience of rejecting something to which those relations might lead is not an authentic, a whole experience of sex.

Sexual intercourse is a total self-giving. We cannot give ourselves totally and hold something back at the same time. We can not give ourselves entirely to the experience of what is there while at the same time refusing to accept everything that is there.

Would this mean that using some method of birth control would make sexual relations inauthentic even within marriage?

Not necessarily. Methods of birth control and family limitation differ, of course. Some are acceptable and some are not. And some methods do have a definitely negative effect on the way couples experience the act of intercourse. But there is a difference between the attitude a married couple can take toward pregnancy, even while trying to avoid it, and the attitude of unmarried couples. Within the relationship of marriage, whether people use some form of birth control for a time or not, sex is never completely separated from its purpose of giving new life.

Openness to new life

In marriage two people are united in a covenant which by its very nature is ordained and open to new life. Both their love for one another and their sexuality are committed to the giving of new life. Their whole relationship to each other is consecrated by their acceptance to give their flesh for the life of the world.

Every act of intercourse does not have to give life biologically. But within the relationship of marriage, every act of intercourse, if it helps parents to love each other more deeply, helps them give life to each other and to the children already in the home. Love helps people—especially children—to grow, to become more fully alive.

Just giving birth, beautiful as it is, is only one element in the process of giving life to children. Everything that helps a child grow to full maturity—emotionally, intellectually, spiritually—is lifegiving. That is why the relationship between adopted children and their parents is so real: The parents who bring a child to maturity through love are more truly the parents of that child than the parents who only gave physical birth.

The home, then, is an extension of the womb. It is a place for children to come to life, to develop, to grow. And the love of a father and mother for each other does more than anything else to make the home an atmosphere of love and of life.

That is why any act of intercourse between married people, if it is an authentic expression of love, is procreative by its very nature. It helps give life to children born and yet unborn.

Even couples who cannot have children because of old age or sterility know that their every act of intercourse identifies them with the lifegiving activity of the whole human race. They are open to children; they have established a family able to receive them. They are doing nothing to deny or to refuse the full meaning and value of their sexual relations; they are giving themselves to everything that is there. And therefore their relationship to one another is authentic, as is the expresssion of their sexuality within it.

But sexual relations outside of marriage have no real connection with the giving of new life. The unmarried have neither the desire nor the right to bring a child into this world. They are unwilling to provide the environment—to establish the family—that a child needs in order to come to full life. Their sexual expression to each other may seem for awhile to enrich the lives of the partners, but usually this is deceptive and short-lived. Outside of marriage sexual relations are by their very nature self-enclosed, open to nothing but the private purposes of the individuals involved.

That is why the whole world celebrates a marriage; but nobody celebrates an affair.

9.

The Challenge of the 'Sexual Revolution'

Sex as social involvement

Having looked at sex as a physical reality, let's look at it now as an element of our culture.

Culturally, the opportunities for interaction between men and women are all but limitless. Eveverything contained in the word *masculinity* or *femininity* is something we can draw on when we express ourselves to others. Masculine and feminine traits enrich a relationship, make it more interesting, exciting and alive. It is not only good to be a man or a woman; it is good to share that goodness with others.

In this chapter, we focus on just one of the bubbles in the boiling pot of present-day interaction between men and women. It is not the most beautiful bubble, nor the richest one to develop, but it is one we have to face. It is the cultural phe-

nomenon of our changing attitude toward premarital sex.

What has been going on in this country, say
the journalists, is a sexual revolution. Traditional
moral values have been challenged in the name of
sexual liberation.

It is certainly true that a lot more sexual
activity is taking place between unmarried people
today than was going on 20 years ago. And a lot
more people are saying it's okay.

It is also true that the revolution is partly the
journalists' making.

The news media can make a pop hero almost
overnight. Press coverage can produce fads—and
even sociological trends—just by giving millions of
people the same idea. The first man to hijack an
airplane had an original idea. The news media gave
that idea to the general population, and now you
cannot board a plane anywhere in the world without going through a security check.

This is no criticism of the news media—just a
comment on how easily we let ourselves be led.
Illogical as it might be, human beings draw great
security from doing what everyone else is doing.
"If everyone says it's okay, it can't be all that bad"
is a common human assumption.

Totalitarian governments know this, and so
the first thing they do when they seize power is try
to make everyone believe that the whole population is solidly behind the new regime. The press is
not allowed to report any opposition except to say
that the people have already rallied behind the government to stamp out the dissidents. The leader's
picture is hung in all public places, and a cult of

personal veneration is drummed up. Anyone who disagrees with the party line is made to believe he is the only one, or almost the only one, who has any doubts about it, and that he must be disloyal, unenlightened, or a freak.

We see the same principle working all around us. Somebody claps, everybody claps. Nobody claps, everyone is afraid to start the applause.

The sexual revolution dates—in the press, at least—from the middle 1960's. Statistically, the change in sexual morals actually began after World War I, but it didn't skyrocket until everyone started hearing about it.

A woman who graduated from high school in 1966 told me how it was when she entered college at the height of the revolution: "The Kinsey report had gotten around. The general argument was, 'How can it be so wrong if everybody is doing it?' You were made to feel guilty if you didn't— like you were hung up or something. But the guilt everybody talked about was the guilt trip the Church had laid upon us, or our parents. Our parents were hung up on sex, or we thought they were, and on a lot of other things. We didn't want to be like them. So we just did the opposite."

And she summed it all up in these words: "We wanted at all costs to be ourselves—to be individuals. So we all just turned around and became individuals together!"

That really does sum it up: Even to be individuals we need the support of a crowd!

The challenge of the sexual revolution comes down to this: Do we let ourselves be swept along with the current, or do we take a personal stand?

How should we—as individuals and as Christians—respond to the sexual stance of our culture?

First, we should recognize that our culture has no single sexual stance. Our culture has more currents in it going more different directions than the waters of the Mississippi River.

On the one hand, we are idealistic about sex. We see it as the expression of love, of an interpersonal relationship. We don't want to exploit others through it, to use people just as objects.

At the same time we are crude about sex, even cynical. We use sexual words as expletives, tell gross sexual jokes, treat irreverently those who come across to us as "sexy," and are undisciplined in our thoughts, our reading, our behavior.

In all this we affect one another. The stance we as individuals take toward sex helps determine what the stance of our culture will be toward sexuality.

In James Dean's movie, *Rebel Without a Cause*, a group of teenage couples on a date were playing "chicken" by racing their cars toward the edge of a cliff. The driver who stopped first was the chicken. James Dean and the boy he was racing against both went too far to stop. Dean jumped out of his car at the last moment.

The driver in the other car went over the edge.

If a group of people who identify with one another start to move in a certain direction—whether toward drug abuse, "sexual freedom" or anything else—some of the members of that group may be able to stop before they get into trouble. But all share responsibility for the ones who go over the cliff.

The casualties

We have already seen the casualty list of the sexual revolution—one million pregnant teenage girls every year, 1.3 million abortions, 600,000 babies conceived out of wedlock. But that is only part of the picture.

Teenagers are only a part of the sexual revolution. And the United States, while also only a part of it, cannot close its eyes to the influence American culture has all over the world.

All revolutions cost something, usually human lives. Who is dying for our sexual liberation? What is the price of sexual freedom? And who pays that price?

Forty million babies every year—that is the number of abortions worldwide.

This is the real fruit of the sexual revolution. What our society has done as a result of increased sexual activity and the resulting epidemic of pregnancies is to decree a new attitude about life itself: Babies in the womb are no longer considered human. They can be cut out like cancer and not even buried—just thrown away with the surgical waste.

This means that worldwide more than five times as many babies are disposed of through abortion every year than the total number of Jews and Christians who were slaughtered by Hitler in the concentration camps during the whole of World War II.

The comparison between our society and Hitler's Germany is worth looking into. If history does not teach us anything, then a lot of people have died in vain.

We say of babies in the womb exactly what Hitler said of the Jews and Slavic peoples during World War II: They are simply not developed enough to be considered human. Hitler's word was *Untermenschen*—sub-humans. We use the words *fetuses* and *pieces of tissue*. It is the same argument. Hitler used it to justify his killing; we use it to justify ours.

Hitler saw the Jews as his social problem. Abortionists see unwanted pregnancy—babies in the womb—as our social problem.

We also use the same propaganda method Hitler used to soften the shock of all this killing on public opinion. We adjust our vocabulary. Hitler never spoke of killing Jews; he talked about a "final solution" to the "Jewish problem." There were no death camps, just "resettlement centers."

We talk about the "problem of unwanted pregnancy" and "removing the fetus." We do not set up centers to kill babies; they frequently are not even called abortion clinics. Our disposal centers go by such names as "Aware Woman Clinic," the "Center for Reproductive and Sexual Health," and the "Feminist Women's Health Center."

The Nazis set up teams of Special Action Groups (*Einsatzgruppen*) to carry out the extermination of the Jews. Their methods are part of the court record of the Nuremberg Trials. Otto Ohlendorf, who was in charge of an *Einsatz* group in the Ukraine, estimates the number of deaths of men, women and children that he presided over in a single year at 90 thousand.

He describes a typical operation: "They [the Jews] were transported to the place of executions, usually an antitank ditch, in trucks. . . . Then they were shot, kneeling or standing, by firing squads in a military manner and the corpses thrown into the ditch. I never permitted the shooting by individuals, but ordered that several of the men should shoot at the same time in order to avoid direct personal responsibility. Other group leaders demanded that the victims lie down flat on the ground to be shot through the nape of the neck. I did not approve of these methods."

Asked "Why not?" Ohlendorf replied, "Because, both for the victims and for those who carried out the executions, it was, psychologically, an immense burden to bear" (William L. Shirer, *The Rise and Fall of the Third Reich*, Fawcett, 1960).

The psychological burden of killing so many human beings in cold blood had observable physical and psychological effects on the SS men who carried out the executions, reports John Toland in his book *Adolf Hitler:* "Some enlisted men had nervous breakdowns or took to drinking, and a number of the officers suffered from serious stomach and intestinal ailments" (Ballantine Books: 1977).

Dr. Bernard Nathanson, once a militant crusader for abortion on demand and former head of New York's Center for Reproductive and Sexual Health (the "busiest licensed abortion facility in the western world"—over 3000 a month in peak season), reports the effect of mass abortions on his clinic staff in almost the same terms ("Second Thoughts on Abortion," *Good Housekeeping*, March, 1976).

Doctors began "losing their nerve in the operating room," Nathanson says. "I remember one sweating profusely, shaking badly, nipping drinks between procedures." Heavy drinking became a problem with several. Some doctors and nurses complained of deep depression, and some were plagued by terrifying recurring nightmares. One doctor's worried wife cornered Nathanson at a party and anxiously reported that her husband was dreaming continually of blood.

"I was seeing personality structures dissolve in front of me on a scale I had never seen before in a medical situation," he recalls. "Very few members of the staff seemed to remain fully intact through their experiences."

Fruits of the revolution

The question we have to ask ourselves is not only what the effect of abortion is on the babies whose lives are terminated in their mothers' wombs. We have to ask about the effect of mass abortion on ourselves, on our whole society. What kind of nation are we creating by these things?

The problem does not begin with abortion; we have to be clear about that. Above all, it does not begin with the poor woman or girl who, in a moment of fear, desperation or confusion, accepts the solution our society so smilingly holds out to her. Those who have abortions are victims just as truly as the children who die—victims of our society.

The problem begins farther back—with the attitude we take toward the nature and use of sex itself.

If we just see sex as a here-and-now thing, a

116

meaningful experience for the moment, then why not see the fetus in the same way, a here-and-now thing, an isolated piece of tissue, instead of as a living body visibly designed by God to grow to the fullness of human life?

If we don't look ahead in sex—to the purpose for which sex was designed—why look ahead in pregnancy to the purpose for which a fetus exists?

But let us be careful: When we stop being aware of the purpose in things, and stop respecting that purpose, we have lost the key to human life. The next step will be to stop looking ahead in our understanding of our own lives—to the purpose life itself is given for.

After 18 months as head of the world's largest abortion facility, during which 60,000 abortions were performed at the clinic, Dr. Nathanson resigned. He had become convinced, he says in the *Good Housekeeping* article, that abortion "is the taking of human life," and that what we are doing to babies is doing even worse to ourselves: "I said to myself: 'All that propaganda you've been spewing out about abortion not involving the taking of human life is nonsense. If that thing in the uterus is *nothing*, why are we spending all this time and money on it?' "I became convinced that as director of the clinic, I had in fact presided over 60,000 deaths."

After World War II every German had to face up to the question of his or her own responsibility for what happened under Hitler. The people in the concentration camps were not killed just by the men who pulled the trigger or dropped the crystals of Zyklon B into the gas chambers. They were killed, with varying degrees of responsibility, by every person who went along with the popular sentiment against Jews or supported Hitler's dream of world conquest.

And the 40 million babies whose lives are terminated each year by abortion as a result of our sexual revolution, and their mothers whose lives will be forever overshadowed by memory—have we no responsibility for them?

How will we feel about our own share in the sexual revolution when we begin to reflect on the price others paid for the liberation we enjoyed—those who went over the cliff?

The sexual revolution is a fact. And our society's method for exterminating the babies who inevitably result from people's enjoyment of their new-found sexual freedom is a significant measure of the revolution. If we agree to become part of the revolution, we have to accept our share of responsibility for all of its consequences.

This is a sobering thought. For some it may be a depressing thought. But it need not be.

We do not have to be a part of the sexual revolution. We can make our own revolution. We have the freedom to choose our own attitudes, to pursue the ideals of sexual behavior we believe in. We can pitch our ideals as high as we desire.

Taking a stand

We will inevitably fail—and many times—to live up to our ideals. But there is all the difference in the world between failing to live up to an ideal and taking sides against it, or just giving up.

Sexual integrity has never been easy for human beings. Our society makes it harder, no doubt, than it has to be. But every person who thinks, speaks and tries to act in a way that supports the true meaning and value of sexuality makes it easier for everyone else. If we show our respect for the sacredness of human life and never act in a way that ignores the connection between sexual enjoyment and the commitment to give new life, we make it easier for everyone else to believe in and work toward a rational use of sex as an ideal.

I once heard a college girl say, "I wouldn't have sex before marriage myself, but I wouldn't put down anyone who does."

That's a cop-out.

If by "putting down" someone else, she meant thinking she was better than the other, or that the other person was evil and guilty, she was right. No one has the right to judge another's guilt.

But I think she meant more than that. I believe she was saying that she wouldn't judge the other person's action; that, as far as she was concerned, if another person wanted to have sex outside of marriage, that was all right with her.

How many people would say, "I wouldn't leave a fire untended in a national forest myself, but I wouldn't put down anyone who does"? Or, "I wouldn't kill little babies myself, but I respect your right to kill them if you want to"?

Anyone who helps establish a trend toward dissociating the pleasure of sex from the purpose of sex is contributing to a situation that affects the life of every person in the country.

I have talked to one male student after another who begins a date with all the best intentions

119

in the world. But once he realizes that the girl he is with is willing, he is just unable to hold back.

On girls the pressure is even worse. As one teenager put it: "Girls want to know how to say no without losing their boyfriend or becoming unpopular. Most parents don't realize how much pressure there is on a girl to prove her love by having sex. We want to know how to handle all that—how to keep dating, be accepted, have boyfriends, without being forced to use sex" (Thomas W. Klewin, "Teenage Pregnancy," *St. Anthony Messenger*, May, 1978).

No man is an island. Everything people do in a society influences other people. And when a particular way of acting becomes so widespread that it turns into a sociological movement—such as the sexual revolution in our day, for example—then for any individual to go against the trend can become as difficult as swimming against the tide.

Someone must take a stand.

And that is a good note to end on, because it gives us somewhere to begin.

10.

Sex as the Expression of Love

The meaning of love is commitment

Giving life is one value in sex. But there is another value, one more immediate to the actual moment of sexual relations, to the act of intercourse itself: Sex is the expression of love.

This is easy to say. Just about everyone does say it, in fact. But it can lead in different directions.

In the middle of the sexual revolution I came back from Africa and began giving retreats in this country. Most of what follows in this chapter came from thinking about what young people told me during those retreats.

Whenever someone talked to me about having had sex on a date, I would ask, "Was this something you did just for the fun of it, or was it with someone you really love?"

If the person answered, "It was with someone I really love," my next question was, "Do you really think this was wrong?"

I was surprised at first how many times younger people, especially girls, would answer, almost with relief that the question had been asked, "You know, I really can't feel there is anything wrong with it. I mean, it's really someone I love and it just seems like the natural thing to do."

My first response to this was to give the answer I had been taught—an answer I had thought about, understood and which I see as a true one: "Sex is for giving life. You don't have a right to the pleasure of sex unless you respect the purpose for which it is designed."

To my great surprise, the answer usually was, "I wasn't doing it for pleasure. I was expressing love."

I must admit, I never got this answer from a male. Males always do it for pleasure. They may do it for love also, but the pleasure alone is enough to make them want to. Whether a man loves or not, there is always pleasure in the act—or he is incapable of having intercourse. This makes men very conscious of how much of their motivation in sex is physical. And they are usually frank about it, at least when talking to other men.

But women are different. For a woman, sex may or may not be all that enjoyable on a given occasion. She may or may not find much physical pleasure in it. For a woman who loves, however, there is always meaning in the act: It is always the expression of love.

A woman who is not in love may have sex for

other reasons. She may just seek the physical pleasure of sex and indulge in it for this alone. But most of the women and girls that I have spoken with who engage in sex without love do it for more than pleasure. They are seeking at least an illusion of love.

As one young woman in her 20's told me: "I know it's not love. But if you can't have the real thing, you're sometimes willing to settle for its image."

Sex for her was more a feeling of security than an intense, physical passion. When she spoke of it, it was not intercourse she remembered; it was waking up and feeling a man's strong back in the bed with her. It was knowing someone was there.

Alice Lake's article "A Girl's Right to Say No" in *Seventeen* (June, 1974) lists four reasons why girls have sex when they really do not want to. Some do it to be popular; some because they are insecure and sex makes them feel wanted; some because of the competition—other people are doing it and they are afraid they will lose their boyfriends if they don't. And the fourth reason is one I have run into again and again: They do not want to hurt the boy's feelings.

The first three reasons are a form of prostitution, and prostitutes are almost always victims. A girl who gives her body as a means to something else—popularity, keeping her boyfriend, relief from insecurity—has no illusions about sex. She is using it as the one thing of value she has for barter. We have all had enough experience of insecurity and loneliness to know this temptation. We are not likely to throw the first stone.

123

In dealing with people on retreats or in confession, I find no problem with people who know they are doing wrong. When we know we are doing wrong, we do not need to hear arguments about the value of what we are sinning against, whether it be sex or anything else. We need encouragement, compassion and a sense of the forgiveness of God. We need help to find a way out.

But what do you say to a person who only wants to give an expression of love? Or who does not want to say no to her boyfriend because he is asking for an expression of her love?

Is it wrong to express love? And if sex is an expression of love, why is it wrong to have sex with someone you really love?

And what is the difference between loving someone and just liking him or her a lot?

This thing called love

What is love?

Is it a feeling? Is it caring about somebody? Is it a "happening"? Is it a choice?

When I was teaching high school, the senior girls in my marriage class used to ask, "How can you know when you love someone enough to marry him?"

It took me two years to realize this was the wrong question.

To start by asking, "How can you know?" is to treat love as if it were just something "there"— just a fact, like a negative or positive reaction to penicillin, like having six toes or not having six toes.

Could we take a *Reader's Digest* 20-Questions

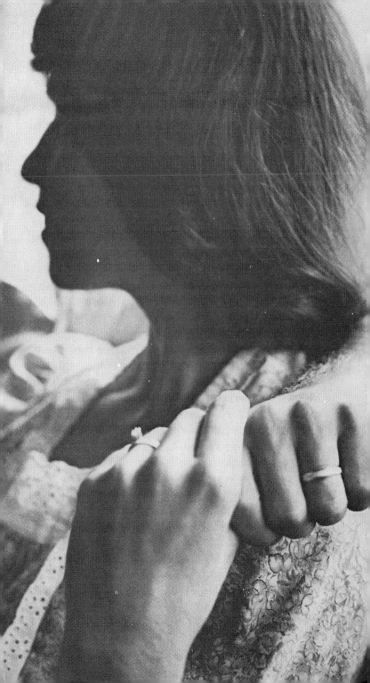

Quiz, for example, to find out whether we love someone? "If your score is 18 or over, marry the person; if 14 to 16, wait; if under 14, don't see each other again!"

Love is a free gift of self to another. Can we start with that?

If love is free—and a gift—it is something that is in our power to give or not to give. Love is a free choice.

It is a free choice of relationship. And it is through relationships that we create ourselves as persons. That is why love is an act on the level of person.

Liking someone is not a free choice. If a boy told a girl his cousin was coming into town and wanted to date her, could she promise to like his cousin—sight unseen?

No, because liking is on the level of emotions, and emotions are not free. We cannot promise to have a reaction we are not free to command.

But we can promise to love. People do promise to love one another for the rest of their lives when they marry. God even made love a commandment. As Jesus said:

" 'You shall love the Lord your God
with your whole heart,
with your whole soul,
and with all your mind.'
This is the greatest and first commandment.
The second is like it:
'You shall love your neighbor as
yourself.' " (Matthew 22:37-38, from
Deuteronomy 6:45 and Leviticus 19:18)
God cannot command—and no one can prom-

ise—what a person is not free to give. If love can be commanded and promised, we must be free to give it to whomever we please. Love must be a free choice, not an automatic physical or cultural reaction. It is something that belongs to the personal level of our being, a free response.

I once had a young couple come to me to get married. Both had been reared Catholics. The girl said she still was, "sort of." The boy said he no longer believed in God.

I asked the young man if he would be willing to talk about the God problem. After all, what you believe about God has a great deal of influence on your life, and two people who intend to spend the rest of their lives together should take that into consideration.

We had some good conversations sitting in his apartment. The upshot was that he had no particular reason for not believing in God, no problem that called for a solution or question to which he could not find an answer. As he put it: "I would like to believe in God; I would love to, in fact. But I just don't. I've read books, talked to people. I know all the arguments; I see the strength of them. But I just don't believe. I wish I did."

He taught me something. His problem had nothing to do with God. It was a problem of human freedom. He did not know he was free to believe or not to believe.

We got to a point in our discussions where he said: "I see that if there is no God the world is absurd. There is no explanation for how it got here; no explanation for what we see and understand it to be. Life itself doesn't make sense. But maybe

127

that's the case. Maybe everything is absurd. I can live with that."

This is not the place to take up the problem of faith: what it is, what it is not, and what it takes to make an act of faith. We just want to note one fact: Faith is a free choice on our part. It is like taking a friend's word for something: No matter how much evidence there is that our friend is telling the truth, ultimately we are free to trust or not to trust. The young man I was talking to could not see that he was free to decide to accept the evidence for God's existence if he wanted to. He could not see that faith was a free choice.

I finally wound up telling the couple that I would marry them, but that in my opinion the marriage would be invalid. For a valid marriage both parties have to commit themselves for life.

"Why wouldn't our marriage be valid?" the young man asked me. "I believe in permanent commitment. I intend to make one."

"Because you don't believe you are free," I answered. "Right now you say that you don't have faith; that you would like to believe, that you have looked for faith, but that you just don't have it. It just 'isn't there.'

"There is no reason why you shouldn't come back in a year or so and say the same thing about love. Faith and love are both ultimately free choices. Suppose you come back and tell me you just don't love this girl anymore—that you would like to love her, you have tried to love her, you have done everything you can to love her, but that love just 'isn't there' anymore. What then?"

No one can promise what he or she is not free

to give. And no one can give what is not under personal control. If love is not something we are free to give, something that depends on our own free choice, then we can never promise to love another person for life. All we can do is say how we feel right now and hope that it lasts!

But marriage vows are a promise, not a prediction.

The young man in the story was actually making a choice—two of them, in fact. He was choosing to refuse freedom, and he was choosing to accept absurdity. And his choices were creating him. He chose to be a person who could accept the world and his own being as irrational, a person who accepted not being free. Even the decision not to choose is a choice that creates us as persons.

The great thing about love is that it is a choice, and a choice that creates us as persons. When we choose to love another person, we choose to enter into a relationship with that other that will help determine who we are. If the relationship is for life, then we are choosing to form, to shape ourself as a person for the rest of our life in response to this other.

This means that *love is a commitment*. It is more than a feeling and, ultimately, independent of whatever feelings there may or may not be.

This gives love its dignity, its value, its significance in our lives. Love is not just a happening. It is not just a chemical reaction or a psychological response. Love is a free human act. We relate to another person in love because we *want* to—that is, because we *choose* to want to, which means a lot more than just being attracted.

129

The difference between liking and loving

Commitment makes the difference between loving and just liking.

As long as we are attracted to each other, we like each other—but we are not committed. If we love each other, however, we are committed; and to live up to that commitment is love, whether we always *feel* attracted to each other or not.

Feelings come and go, but love remains. As long as two people are attracted to each other, they can talk about liking one another. But when they commit themselves, they can begin to speak about love.

Love, therefore, is not just any kind of relationship. It is a committed relationship.

Few of us would say that, all of the time, we really *like* our brothers and sisters—or even, sometimes, our parents. But we can say we *love* the other members of our family, because we know there is a mutual bond of commitment between us so strong that we would never break it.

No one would say he or she likes every other person in the world. But if someone is willing to serve others generously—even to die for others—then that person loves his or her fellow human beings.

A husband and wife do not always appear to like each other as much as two young people who are dating. They are not always talking to each other on the phone or trying to get a glimpse of one another. Yet there is a depth to their relationship that comes from their mutual commitment. They have given themselves to one another in an enduring bond of love.

Commitment is what gives security to love. We are only secure in relationships with others whose love for us is not just an attraction, but a commitment. And then our security is only as strong as our belief in the other's word.

Why are we secure in the love of our parents, of our brothers and sisters whom at times we may even feel we don't like? It is because we know that, whatever might happen, and however our family might feel about us, they will never let us down—not if we really need them.

If we were to get sick, become invalids, require constant attention for the rest of our lives, our parents would take care of us. And if our parents died, our brothers and sisters would take over. That is what love is: a relationship you can count on; a commitment as deep and radical as the level of human freedom itself.

When Jill Kinmont broke her neck on the mountain and was paralyzed for life, her fiance broke off the engagement. He had wanted—intended—to marry her. But he was not committed. When she became a paralytic, he changed his mind about taking her as his wife.

Actually, he was free to change his mind, whether or not we admire him for being the kind of person who would do so. He had not yet *committed* himself to loving Jill Kinmont for the rest of his life; he was only planning to make a commitment. Both he and Jill knew that either one of them was free to reconsider and back out.

That is the difference between engagement and marriage: In marriage, commitment is a fact.

To understand love as a commitment makes the strength of love depend not on what the other person might do or become, but on the substance of one's own soul. To love is to commit one's self to a relationship with the other. Not to endure in that commitment is to deny one's very self—not just to the other, but in the depth of one's own soul. To go back on a commitment is not just to refuse one's self; it is—in part, at least—to lose one's self. It is a failure to be free. And freedom is what the self is all about.

The real value of freedom lies in the fact that through our free choices we create ourselves as persons. And this brings out the value of commitment: A commitment is a free choice that endures.

When we commit our love to another and fail to live up to that commitment, we fail to be the self we have chosen to be, the self we ourselves have determined to identify—in great or small part, at least—with relationship to the other. We take back the word of our own self-creation.

When we ask a question about love, then, we are asking less about what the other person is for us—how the other person affects us, whether he or she is able to "turn us on"—than we are about ourselves. The real question to ask in love is how we choose to give ourselves to the other: what we are willing to commit, how definitively we are willing to commit it.

Love is a decision to be committed.

My senior girls asked me the wrong question: "How can you know when you love a boy enough to marry him?" And I didn't know how to answer it. What I should have answered was, "You don't ask whether you love him enough to marry him; you ask whether you can commit yourself to him for life in all the ways that married love implies, and whether you want to do this. If you do want to, and feel you can, then you can love him. If you actually make that commitment—and live up to it—then you do love him.

And the strength of your love will be the measure of your soul.

From the young people who told me that for them sex was the expression of love, I learned a whole new dimension of the value of sexual relations. I learned it, not just from the words themselves, but from thinking about what those words had to mean: If sex is the expression of love, and the essence of love is commitment, then sex must be the expression of commitment.

To say that—and understand what it means—gives a whole new dimension to sex. It makes sex an expression of the will, a word of commitment made flesh.

Sex is the expression of a pledge. But what kind of commitment—what kind of pledge—do sexual relations express?

11.

Sex as Symbolic Language
Sex is a pledge of spousal love

Sex is the expression of love. But sex is obviously not the expression of every kind of love. No one would have sexual relations to express love for parents, or brothers or sisters, for example.

So what kind of love do sexual relations express? And is there any intrinsic connection between the kind of love that is being expressed and the particular gestures—the gestures of sexual relations—which express it?

What makes sex an expression of commitment? Did somebody just decide one day that it would be? Or is there something about sexual relations themselves that make them expressive of the gift of self?

To answer these questions, we have to decide what makes one kind of love differ from another.

What makes love of parents differ from love of one's fellow countrymen? What is the difference between the love we have for our brothers or sisters, or for our best friends, and the love we give to a husband or wife? Is there a difference between the love of engaged couples and the love those same people will have for each other when they are married?

What makes the difference? Sure, in each of these relationships we like or we love the other person in a different kind of way. But what makes each way of loving someone different?

Is it the way we feel about the other person? It is true that we feel differently about our parents, our friends, and the people we date. Husbands and wives have a different feeling toward each other than they have toward their children. But if we are just talking about feelings, we are not talking about love. We have already seen that love is essentially not a feeling but a commitment. So different kinds of love must mean different kinds of commitment.

Feelings usually go with love; but they are not the reality of love. We can have good feelings without real love, and we can have real love without constantly experiencing good feelings. In fact, until love has been tested by the absence of feelings for awhile, we cannot really be sure that we love.

Feelings, then, are not the reality of love any more than enjoying a good meal is the reality of eating. Usually those who love feel deeply toward each other. And usually people who eat enjoy it. But with or without the feeling, eating is eating, and love is love. So we can't identify love by our feelings.

What, then, is the difference—the real difference—between the love we have for our parents, for our friends, for those we date, and for the person we marry?

The difference lies in what we commit to each person. All love is a commitment. What we commit determines the kind of love we give.

Toward our parents we have certain commitments, which we acknowledge and respect. They may not be spelled out in great detail, but the general drift of them is expressed pretty well in the commandment, "Honor your father and your mother. . ." (Exodus 20:2) and "My son, take care of your father when he is old. . ." (Sirach 3:12).

The commitment we have toward our friends would be much harder to spell out. It differs with each friend. It is more implicit than explicit. It is just that we know there are certain things we have a right to expect or to count on from each other because of our friendship. Whatever these things are, they constitute the implicit commitment of the friendship. Real friends are not just people we like to be with; they are the people we know we can count on and who know they can count on us. The commitments we have toward one another, vague and undefined as they might be in our minds, are the real substance of our friendships.

Spousal love—the love married persons commit to one another—is a very particular kind of commitment. It differs from the love of friends for one another, or from the love of parents for children and children for parents. It is even different from the love of people who are dating one another or who are engaged.

Spousal love, the love of husband and wife, is essentially a commitment to total union. Spouses commit themselves to do all those things which, by their very nature, tend to bring two people to total union of mind and will and heart.

A husband and wife are committed to growing toward union of mind. This means they are committed to talking with each other, to communicating with each other as deeply as they can all of their lives in an effort to arrive at perfect understanding of one another.

They are also committed to growing toward union of wills—toward agreeing on what they should do, accepting each other's ideals, giving up all selfishness in an effort to be pleasing to one another.

And if they live with each other long enough, and share enough experiences—happy, tragic, challenging, comic—they will eventually grow into a harmony of heart, into a certain sympathy even on the emotional level that helps them be totally one. A union of hearts, too, is something to which they are committed.

Spousal love, then, is a commitment—a pledge—to spend the rest of one's life doing with another all of those things that of themselves tend to lead two persons to perfect union of mind and will and heart. It is a real gift of self.

The key word here is *union.* Spouses, married people, are committed to work at becoming one with each other: one in understanding; one in their goals; one in attitudes and values, in their ideals and deepest feelings, insofar as this can be; two in one flesh.

Keeping commitments straight

Spousal love is not a commitment to love husband or wife *more* than other people. Does a wife love her husband more than her children? Does a man necessarily love his wife more than his own mother and father, his brothers and sisters?

No, the love between husband and wife is just a different kind of love—because of what husband and wife commit to one another. And love for parents is a different kind of love. So is love for one's children, or for one's brothers and sisters, or for one's fellow human beings.

Ideally, we shouldn't have to talk about loving anyone more than another, because God has taught us we should love all people perfectly.

If love is a commitment, and if we keep our commitments clear, we don't have to ask whom we love more or less. We just have to know what we have committed to each different person in love.

Marriage, for example, is a commitment to perfect openness with one another. Married people are pledged to communicate deeply and totally, in order to achieve perfect union of mind and heart. Talking deeply to one another for the rest of each one's life is implied in the marriage vows.

But parents do not have this commitment with regard to their children, or children with regard to their parents. Our fathers do not share with us all of the thoughts, feelings, hopes, fears, or anxieties that they share with our mothers. This is not because they love us less; it is just because they have that kind of relationship—and commitment—with our mothers, and not with us.

Likewise, we do not tell our parents all of the things that go on in our hearts. But we will tell them to our husbands or our wives. And our spouses will have a right to expect this kind of openness from us—as we can expect it from them.

Married couples do not leave home to live together because they love each other more than their families. It is because living together is part of what marriage is all about. Two people can hardly work at becoming one mind and heart and soul with each other if one lives in West Virginia and the other in Chicago.

So when we speak of spousal love, we are speaking, not of *more* commitment, but of a special *kind* of commitment. And sex is the language that expresses this commitment.

Sex is an expression of each one's total gift of self to the other. It makes love vivid and real. It can turn tears into laughter, anger into tenderness, withdrawal into generous gift of self. It makes people want to be given. It encourages couples to keep trying. In moments of misunderstanding it helps bridge the gap until communication can be restored. A meeting of bodies does much to bring about a meeting of minds.

Sex is intimacy. Sex is openness. Sex is awesome, comical and fun. Above all, sex is a language.

The language of sex

The value of sex is that it is a way of expressing love.

But we all know that sex is not the language to express any and every kind of love. No one would use sex to express love for father or mother,

for brother or sister. Sex is the expression of a particular kind of love.

We have already said, though, that love is commitment. And the different kinds of love are just different sets of commitments. So sex is the expression to another person of a particular set of commitments that one has made or is making to that person.

What are the commitments that sex expresses?

If we look at sex as a language, we can find in the gestures of sex itself the meaning they contain. Sexual touches between human beings are symbolic touches; they are a language of signs.

Human sexual gestures are charged with meaning and with personal self-expression from beginning to end. They are the mutual self-expression of two free, rational, self-orienting, self-bestowing persons. Behind every physical touch, every physical movement of sex, is a free person saying something of himself or herself, saying something to the other, speaking a language of love.

To understand sex as a language is to understand sex on the personal level. And this is to understand the value that sex has in itself.

When I was in Africa I had what one might call a "topless parish." I expected when I went there that this would cause me some problems as a male. What I actually found, however, was that nakedness in Africa was not sexually exciting.

This was especially surprising since the Africans by and large have beautiful figures. When I reflected on all this I began to realize for the first time what sex really is.

"If nakedness over here is not sexually exciting, then what," I asked myself, "is so exciting about nakedness in marriage?"

The answer was very simple: Nakedness in Africa was not sexually exciting because it said nothing. It was taken for granted.

Then nakedness in marriage must be exciting because of what it says. In marriage the nakedness of husband and wife to one another is a symbolic gesture. It is a physical sign of pledge. It is a way of saying, "I promise to be naked in heart and soul to you all of my life."

It is a natural sign, a language all humans can understand. It is a promise of love. And love is what everyone desires.

Nakedness in the context of marriage is a way of saying, "I promise to be open to you all of my life, to share the depths of my heart and soul with you. But since I can't expose my whole soul to you in one act, I will expose my whole body to you as a pledge. I can be completely naked to you in body, and I will be, as a sign of my desire and determination to be completely naked to you in heart and soul for the rest of my life."

Seen this way, the nakedness of marriage is a physical expression of love, of self-gift. It is a way of saying, "I give myself to you. I share my whole self with you."

It is an expression of commitment. Nakedness in marriage would be meaningless if it did not carry with it the promise to talk, to share one's heart and mind with the other, to draw aside the curtains of one's inner life, one's personal depths, one's soul.

The same can be said of all the gestures of sexual gift within marriage. They are physical, symbolic expressions of a promise.

The touches, the intimacy, the erotic caressing that prepares for the sexual act—all these are ways of saying, "With you I will have no reserves. With you there is no place I draw the line. I give my whole person to you." They excite not just physical desire, but desire for total union with a person.

That is why sexual intercourse, which is the total gift and surrender of the body, is by its very nature an expression of the total gift and surrender of one's self.

We cannot give ourselves effectively to another in one act. We are too selfish. There is too much in ourselves that has to be overcome little by little before we can really be totally given to another. But we can give our bodies in one act, as a pledge of our commitment, of our determination to work at giving ourselves completely to the other for the rest of our lives.

This is what sex is: a language of total gift, a language of lifelong commitment, a language of spousal love.

A compelling logic

There is a logic to this chapter—a logic which leads us inevitably if we follow it step-by-step:

1) Sex has personal value.

2) Its value is to be the expression of love.

3) But the reality of love is commitment.

4) Sex, then, is the expression of commitment.

5) Sex does not express just any kind of commitment, however, because we don't use sex to express just any kind of love.

144

6) So what kind of love does sex express? (In Chapter 8 we saw that human sexuality has an obvious, an undeniable relationship to giving life. On the physical level, this is what sexuality is for. Now in this chapter we have seen that, on the personal level, sexual relations are a language. They are physical, symbolic gestures to express a commitment to be one: one in mind, one in will, one in heart.)

7) Only in marriage can sexuality be ordered both to the giving of new life and to a total union of persons.

8) The love that sex expresses, then, is spousal love.

9) And this is the commitment of marriage.

10) Therefore, any truly sexual expression that we give to another person outside of the relationship of committed, married love is simply a lie. Or, it is a deliberate denial of the personal meaning and value of sex.

There is only one exception to this conclusion that I know of. Sometimes people have sex, not as a deliberate anything, but just as an act of passion. They get carried away. They give in.

When this happens to us, we have failed one test. We have failed to act as whole persons, with our emotions, intellects and wills. We have acted on the physical and, perhaps, on the cultural level of our being while failing to act on the other two levels as graced, spiritual persons.

As soon as we fail the test, however, we get a make-up question, which is, "How do you respond to the failure?"

If we justify our failure and say that what we

did was authentic, a legitimate use of sex, then we have done more than succumb to passion. We have chosen consciously to take a position which falsifies and distorts the very meaning and value of sex in our whole lives.

We cannot do this without distorting our own value as persons.

To admit failure, however, and regret it, is the way to regain what we lost. Every time we recognize that sex without commitment is wrong, we reaffirm the value of commitment; we dedicate ourselves anew to the meaning and value that sex should have in our lives.

If sex is the expression of love; and if love is essentially commitment; then sex without commitment is a lie. That's what it all adds up to.

Many people have asked me over the course of the past few years, "Can't we be committed without being married? What difference does a ceremony make?"

Suppose I give my car keys to a friend. I say to my friend, "The car is really yours. I give it to you. I mean it."

Does that car really belong to my friend? Suppose he takes the car out and has a wreck—kills someone because the brakes were bad. Who gets sued?

I do. Everyone knows that. Until the registration papers are filled out in my friend's name, I am the legal owner of that car. I am responsible for its condition and for everyone who drives it.

In other words, we simply cannot give a car away unless we transfer the papers. That's the law.

It is not just a law; it is common sense. It is

reality. Since we ask other people—society, the courts, the judges—to judge between the parties in a lawsuit; and since we ask our government (which, again, means other people) to hold car owners responsible for the safety of their cars, society has to know who a car's real owner is. Without legal documentation this would be impossible.

What about the gift of the body?

Sex is not a purely personal affair; it cannot be. We ask society to intervene in case of rape. We ask the courts to rule on cases of alimony and child support.

If society had no way of knowing whether two people were married or not, all this would be impossible.

Suppose no woman or girl could ever prove she was married except by insisting that this was the understanding between herself and her boyfriend—in her mind, at least—when she consented to go to bed?

Suppose no man could ever claim a child as his own, or have it recognized as his by family and friends, unless the mother agreed that it was his?

As long as we live in human society, or ask our families and friends to be concerned about us, we just can't enter into a relationship as significant as marriage without letting people know.

In other words, we cannot really make the gift of ourselves to another—we can't give our bodies away—unless we are willing to stand up and say it in public.

Commitment is a word with a meaning. To be committed means you have given up the right to change your mind.

As long as two people are free to change their minds about the relationship they have with one another, they are not committed. To say that they are is to deny the very meaning of the word.

And this is true even of engagement.

A seminarian once asked me at a banquet what I thought of pre-ceremonial sex.

"Suppose a couple is going to be married on Saturday morning," he said. "On Friday night they are out together and they decide to go to bed. The next morning they are married. That's 'pre-ceremonial' sex. Would you say it is the same as 'pre-marital' sex?"

At the table with us was a newspaper editor from Florida. He was the father of eight children. He said to the seminarian:

"Well, let's put it this way. You are a deacon now. You are going to be ordained a priest in four months. Suppose the ordination is set for Saturday morning and on Friday night you go out with some friends. They ask you to say Mass for them that night. After all, you're going to be ordained the next morning. If you do say Mass, is that like saying Mass before you are a priest—or is it just a 'pre-ceremonial' Mass?"

"Our sacrament," he added, "makes just as much difference as yours."

Most people know in their hearts that sex outside of marriage is wrong—much as we may tell ourselves or try to tell one another that it isn't. But we are not always able to answer either the questions in our own minds or the objections of those around us. To some extent the culture has confused us. To some extent we pressure one another.

148

The explanation in this book is not going to force anyone to accept an ideal that he or she does not want to accept. It takes more than logic to do that. But I hope this book will provide some answers for those who want or need them, and a justification for restricting sex to marriage.

To refuse to engage in any sexual expression which does not mean—which cannot mean under the circumstances—what sex is intended to mean is not a denial of our sexuality, although many may call it this. It is an affirmation of the true meaning and value of sex. It is an insistence on keeping sex whole.

And that has a lot to do with keeping us whole as persons.

12.

The Value of a Sexual Word
A 'word' is a person made flesh

A college teacher once asked me during a retreat, "Can't sex have a variety of meanings? Can't it mean one thing with one person, something else with another?"

Sex can have a variety of meanings—and it does—but only within the context of its natural meaning—its fundamental symbolism as the expression of committed, spousal love. In marriage sexual relations have all different shades or nuances of meaning because the relationship between the persons is constantly growing and changing even while it remains the same. Sex can be serious, playful, comical and mystical. It can express forgiveness, acceptance, surrender and desire. Sex can have a multitude of meanings. But the basic meaning of spousal commitment must underlie them all.

Since sex by its very nature expresses total, lifelong gift, to have sex with different persons is to deny the essential meaning of sex itself. That is why sex cannot mean one thing with one person and another thing with someone else. Sex with more than one person does not mean anything at all.

The natural symbolism of sex is a basic human gesture; it is a natural "word" of physical, human expression. If we do not mean what the gestures of sex express, we have not changed the meaning of sex; we have denied it.

Some people argue that there is no such thing as an objective, God-given meaning to sex. They would maintain that sexual relations mean anything the persons engaging in them intend them to mean. For some people, they argue, sex might mean total gift; for others it might be just a sign of affection.

Many people say this. I don't think anyone really believes it. *Time* magazine (Nov. 21, 1977) quotes a 25-year-old teacher who lived with her husband Bob for a year before marrying him: "Intellectually," she says, "I think it's fine to sleep around. But emotionally I'd be very, very upset if Bob slept with another woman. I wish I could be more liberated about this."

To be liberated from those emotions she would have to be liberated from the common sense which tells her that sex is not a meaningless gesture. If a man sleeps with a woman, that means something. Intellectually she does not really "think it's fine to sleep around." Her feelings about her husband are proof of that.

The same article quotes the ex-wife of a Chicago psychologist who advocated "open marriage." She took him at his word and had an affair. When he found out, the marriage broke up. Clearly he thought sex meant something too.

What is true of sex after marriage is true of sex before marriage. If we want sexual relations to express the total gift of ourselves to the person we marry, we cannot say that when we have sexual relations before marriage they do not mean this.

The gestures of sex either mean gift or they do not. If we have decided that sometimes they won't mean gift, then we don't recognize the gestures themselves as ever meaning gift.

A gift is not the same as a loan. We either give our bodies in sex or we loan them. Sexual relations can be the expression of only one or the other, not both interchangeably. To say that expressions of sexual intimacy just mean whatever we might want them to mean on any given occasion, or with any particular person, is to take all the meaning out of sexual expression itself.

This is the most radical denial of our sexuality.

We can change our minds about the meaning of sex, of course. The Scriptural word for this is *metanoia* or repentance. It is possible that at one time in our lives we didn't attach much meaning or value to our sexual gestures. Then we come to the point where we do attach great meaning and value to them. But it is not the meaning of sex itself that has changed; we have just been converted to a clearer, deeper understanding of the meaning with which sex is endowed. We have come to appreciate sex for what it really is. *We* have changed.

If we insist, however, that our own sexual gestures might mean total gift or might not, according to our intention, then we are saying that our own sexual words deserve small respect. They are like paper money whose value goes up and down and can never be taken at face value. Then they are not really the immediate expression of our person; they are just an expression which we use—somewhat arbitrarily—to say one thing to one partner now, something else to another partner later.

Then sex and our person are divided. In all of our sexual expression a gap is left between person and gesture—the very gap that sex is meant to bridge. If our person is not really identified with or embodied in the word of our sexual expression, then we are unable sexually to become a word made flesh for another. Our bodies and our souls are not one.

Perhaps to understand this—and the value of sex as a language—we need a deepened appreciation of what it means for a human being to speak a word. We may have forgotten, to some extent, the unity that should exist between a person and his or her word.

One's person, one's freedom and one's word are all very close to being the same. Lose one, and something very significant is lost to the other two.

One of the finest contributions of T.H. White's epic trilogy *The Once and Future King* is his characterization of Lancelot:

> What sort of picture do people have of
> Sir Lancelot from this end of time? Perhaps
> they only think of him as an ugly young
> man who was good at games. But he was

more than this. He was a knight with a medieval respect for honour.

There is a phrase which you sometimes come across in country districts even nowadays, which sums up a good deal of what he might have tried to say. Farmers use it in Ireland, as praise or compliment, saying, "so-and-so has a Word. He will do what he promised."

Lancelot tried to have a Word. He considered it, as the ignorant country people still consider it, to be the most valuable of possessions (Book III, Berkeley Medallion Books, 1966).

In Scripture a man's word is not just a sound he makes or a means of communication. The word expresses the person—in some sense is the person. A person's word carries all the power and energy of his or her being, of personhood.

In this we are like God, who by his spoken word created the heaven and earth (Genesis: 1).

Isaac's word of blessing to his son Jacob, though intended for Esau, cannot be recalled once it is pronounced. It will have its effect (Genesis: 27).

And Jesus, the expression of the Father's own truth and being, is called by St. John the Word of God. By his Incarnation he became the Word-made-flesh.

A human being's sexual act is also a word-made-flesh. It is the embodiment of a person in response. Where the body and the person are one, sex is an incarnate word, it is an act of love made flesh.

155

Words can be used cheaply, of course, but not without loss to the meaning of the words themselves—and to the credibility of the person who uses them. By using words lightly—falsely, superficially, flippantly—we impoverish not just our language but our power of speech. We erode the very earth of our human expression. This is true of our sexual words as well.

That may be why Jesus said, ". . .do not swear at all. . . . Say, 'Yes' when you mean 'Yes' and 'No' when you mean 'No.' Anything beyond that is from the evil one" (Matthew 5:34, 37).

Jesus was concerned not just with speech, but with the value human persons should attach to the expression of themselves through speech. And this is a concern we should share. We should be particularly concerned about the value of our sexual expression. This dimension of ourselves is too important to cheapen.

I once asked a college student to give a talk for me about sex in a high school retreat. I didn't know what she was going to say, but she had been on a retreat with me when she was in high school, and I knew that her perspective would add light.

"When I was in high school," she told the group, "I was dating a boy I really liked. I could say I loved him. We never had intercourse together, but I gave expression, physical expression, to my feelings for him in other ways.

"Now that I'm in college I find I've grown a lot. I experience a lot of things on a level I never knew before. And one of these is love. The boy I'm dating now, I love him in a way that's—well, it's just a level I never knew existed.

"I wish I had saved for the level of love I know now some of the expression I gave to love in high school."

I didn't ask her what she meant; but in some way she was talking about the value of her word—of what she wanted the word of her body to mean when she used it to express herself in love. And she was seeing that sexual words lose some of their meaning when we use them to say less than they are really meant to say.

There is one thing we might misunderstand from her story, however. We might think she meant to say that now that she was experiencing "real" love some sexual gestures of affection would be appropriate, as if the sexual expression of love could have some meaning outside of marriage as long as the degree of expression matches the degree of love one feels.

This would be to miss the whole point. Sex is not a way of expressing more love or less love. It is a way of expressing a particular kind of love, a particular reality of commitment. If that commitment isn't there, then any truly sexual expression of affection is out of place, is a false use of sex, is a denial of the true meaning and value of sex itself.

It is not an authentic use of sex to go farther with someone we like more and not go as far with someone we like less. Sex is not a scoring system. It is a language: the unique, special, exclusive language of spousal love.

The whole language of sex is the language of spousal love. Only those who actually have this relationship to one another can speak the language authentically at all. If we try to use it outside of

158

marriage we will be speaking in a tongue that does not belong to us, that we have no right to use. And to anyone who knows the authentic language of human sexuality, every sexual word we utter will have a hollow sound. It will betray us as trying to pass ourselves off for something we are not.

Within marriage, sexual gestures mean what they say—because all truly sexual gestures, in some way or another, speak of total gift. Outside of marriage no sexual gestures mean what they say; and therefore as expressions of our sexuality they are falsified. They are a contradiction in terms. By seeming to speak of a commitment which in reality is not a fact they distort our experience of sex. They confuse us.

Here you have the problem of premarital sex in a nutshell. We have heard all our lives that sex is the expression of love. We see sex in movies and on TV being used to express something that looks like love—not just when we are shown sexual intercourse, but when we see other gestures and intimacies that are clearly and explicitly acts of sexual stimulation. We begin to draw a parallel between the degree of affection we feel for another—or the other for us—and the amount of sexual stimulation we have a right to give or to claim.

And we do, in fact, begin to claim some sexual gestures as a right, even while dating in high school. We may not use the word, but we make clear to the person we are dating that we will feel hurt or angry if he or she denies us whatever degree of physical intimacy—including some strictly sexual intimacies—we have come to expect as appropriate to the length or depth of our relationship.

This is a total misunderstanding of sex.

Sex is a language; a language of total commitment. No one has a right to expect of us—or we of anyone else—any words of sexual love until total commitment is a fact. And that commitment is not a fact until marriage is a fact, because that is what marriage is: an act of total commitment.

If sex is the expression, not of a particular kind of love—namely, of marital commitment—but just of a greater or lesser degree of love, then there would be no way for someone growing up to know when it is time to express love through sex.

The last stoplight

The girl who spoke to my retreat group thought, when she was in high school, that the love she experienced then was the deepest level there was, "real" love. When she got into college and matured some more she discovered a deeper level of love. And who is to say how many deeper and deeper levels of love she will discover as she matures even more?

Once when I was driving in Schenectady, New York, looking for a retreat house, I stopped at a gas station to ask directions.

"How do I get to Union Street?" I yelled.

"Go straight down this road to the last stoplight," the attendant yelled back. "Then turn right one block and you'll hit it."

I drove past one stoplight after another, wondering which one would be the last. When I finally stopped to ask directions again, I was in Albany.

I've often thought since then that when we tell ourselves that sex is the expression of love—

meaning the last, the ultimate level of affection be-tween man and woman, the "real thing"—we make the same mistake. How are we to know what level is last?

If, in the course of growing up we can have relationships of friendship and love on deeper and deeper levels, each one being the last thing or ulti-mate level in our experience up to then, how are we to know when we have really reached the final level of love's potentiality, or whether there is more to come?

The only solution is to understand sex for what it really is: the expression of a particular kind of commitment rather than of a greater or lesser degree of affection or love.

Then we will draw the line before marriage, not between one level of sexual intimacy and an-other, or one degree of passion and another, but simply between those expressions of affection that are not truly sexual expressions and those that are.

Everything sexual we will save for marriage. Any expression of affection that is not sexual we will give as we feel moved. (For a discussion of sexual and non-sexual expressions of affection, see Chapter 16.)

In this way we will keep the word of our sex-uality real. As persons we will have a word; and in the sexual joy of marriage the word will be made flesh.

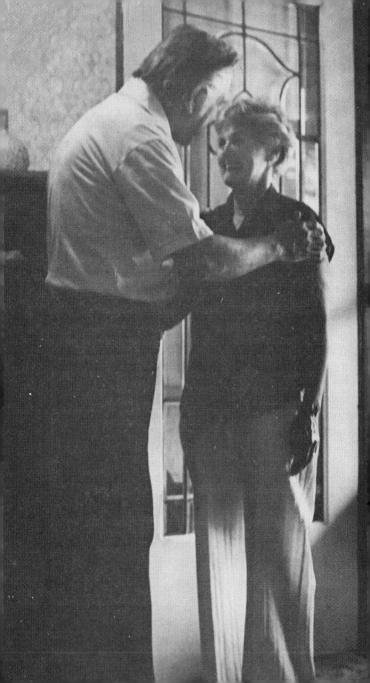

13.

A Word of Enduring Love
The meaning Jesus gave sex and marriage

When we spoke of the four levels of life in Chapter 3, we said that the fullness of life to which Jesus Christ calls his followers extends to our sexual lives, and that Jesus, the Master of the Way, leads us to a height and depth of experience in sex that is not only human but divine.

We claimed that Jesus has something to say about sex which is "good news," something that makes the Christian attitude toward sex different from that of other people in the world.

What is the teaching of Jesus about sex?

"The Word became flesh" (John 1:14)

The first thing Jesus taught us was the value of a word made flesh.

That is what Jesus is—the Word of God made

flesh. God wasn't able just to look down on people from heaven and declare his love to them from a distance. He had to take flesh. He had to come down to earth and take a body to be the expression of himself. He had to let his love for us take the form of physical actions. He could not remain on the level of words alone.

And this is true of us also. We are made in the image of God. We are not content just to speak words of love or of self-revelation to one another. We too have to let our words take flesh. This is natural to us. It is also something we have been taught to understand and appreciate more deeply through Jesus Christ, the Word of God made flesh.

Through his Incarnation—through his becoming flesh—Jesus taught the world the value of letting what is inside of us find expression outside.

It is not enough that we choose something in our hearts; the words of our choices must take flesh in action—in external actions—or our choices will never be fully real. It is not enough that we love someone; we have to express that love externally.

There are many ways to let our words take flesh. Every personal decision that is carried out into action is a word made flesh. We can express love for another by taking time to listen, by helping out with money or service, or just with a pat on the shoulder. But love isn't fully real until it is expressed in some form of action.

"My body. . .given for you" (Luke 22:19)

Sex is a special way of giving physical expression to love. Sex is the expression of love through symbolic gestures—through actions that have sign value.

As we have already seen (Chapters 11 and 12), what gives meaning and value to sex on the level of *person* is the fact that it is the expression of ourselves. Sex is a language. Really to understand sex, and to engage in sex with all of the depth and meaning we should bring to it, we have to understand the language of signs, of symbolic gestures.

But the language of symbolic gestures is something that Jesus of Nazareth, the Master of the Way, understood and spoke to perfection—and teaches us to speak.

The Gospels are full of the sign language of Jesus. He hardly ever cured without touching. He laid his hands on people, put his fingers into the ears of the deaf man, took a dead child by the hand and raised her up. And he taught his followers to express themselves also in signs, in sacraments: water and oil, bread and wine.

But the peak of Jesus's symbolic expression of himself came with the crucifixion.

Christians have always seen in the passion and death of Jesus on the cross an act of self-expression. The Son of God who was made flesh in Jesus chose to give expression to his love for the Father, and for all people, through the gift of his body on the cross.

The crucifixion was a passionate, symbolic, physical gesture of love.

As intercourse is.

It may at first seem a little shocking to us to compare sexual intercourse with the passion and death of Jesus on the cross. But they are basically

165

the same kind of reality: Both are physical, symbolic gestures. Both are expressions of love. Both are passionate: one with the passion of pleasure, the other with the passion of pain. But both are passionate ways of expressing self-gift to another. And both are the expression of commitment.

Jesus gave his body on the cross as a sign that God would be given to his people forever. In the crucifixion, God pledged himself: Christ's blood was the seal of a covenant.

And that is what intercourse is: a pledge of unending self-gift, the seal of a covenant that will last until death.

In the crucifixion the body of Jesus was naked, his heart opened by the soldier's lance as a sign that the heart of Christ—his deepest thoughts and desires, all that the Father had made known to him—would be open and revealed to us forever.

And the nakedness of intercourse is another way of pledging exactly the same thing.

When Jesus himself—at the Last Supper—wanted to teach his apostles the meaning of the passion and death he was about to undergo, he took bread, broke it and gave it to them saying, "This is my body, which will be given up for you."

And this is what each person is saying to the other in intercourse: "This is my body, which is given up for you."

Sexual intercourse is a gift of one's body to the other in love. It is the sign of a gift of self that aspires to be as total as that of Jesus on the cross.

"My flesh for the life of the world" (John 6:51)

Through intercourse two people are pledging

166

themselves to all that their lives together will demand of them in love. They are likewise committing themselves to all of the children who will be born of their love. They do not know in advance all that may be asked of them. But they commit themselves all the same, holding nothing back.

In both of these commitments their promise is to be life-giving. They are pledging to give life to one another—deeper, richer, fuller life—through the relationship they promise to maintain. And they are pledging to be life-giving to their children, not only in the physical sense, but in all the ways that parenthood offers and demands.

Intercourse between married people is a way of saying with Christ, "My flesh, for the life of the world."

"He. . .would show his love for them to the end" (John 13:1)

Through his crucifixion Jesus brought another depth of meaning to the symbolic gesture of sex: the ideal of irrevocable commitment. Jesus exalted sex into the expression of a gift of self as absolute as his own; a gift that can never be taken back.

In our day, when divorce is so common that it is almost taken for granted, we are liable to forget that Jesus abolished it for Christians. He changed the teaching of Moses in this respect.

The Jewish law allowed divorce under certain circumstances. But when Jesus was asked, "May a man divorce his wife for any reason whatever?," he replied that married people are "no longer two but one flesh. Therefore, let no man separate what God has joined."

As for the divorces allowed by the law, Jesus explained: "Because of your stubbornness Moses let you divorce your wives. . . , but at the beginning it was not that way." And he went on to give his new law of marriage: "The man who divorces his wife (lewd conduct is a separate case*) and marries another commits adultery" (Matthew 19: 3-9).

Those who heard Jesus say this found it as shocking—as unrealistic—as we do today to think that a man and woman could commit themselves unconditionally to each other for life, given all the unknowns of each one's personality, all of the ways two human beings can fail one another.

They found this so unrealistic that they told him, "If that is the case between man and wife, it is better not to marry." But Jesus didn't back down. He had made a new reality out of sex and marriage because he had made a new reality out of life itself.

"Life. . .to the full" (John 10:10)

Jesus has given us the Kingdom. He has won for us and promised us the absolute, the total fulfillment of all our capacity for life, for joy, for happiness. He has made available to us the possession and enjoyment of God himself forever.

And so he can say to us that it makes no difference, ultimately, what we have or do not have, what we find or do not find, what we experience or do not experience of created reality in this life.

---

*Literally, "except for porneia." This exception probably referred to marriages that Jews considered incestuous and therefore invalid.

Already we have it all. And we have it now. The treasure hidden in the field. The pearl of great price. The Kingdom.

And so life can be lived on a new basis: not one of preoccupation with getting and securing, with tasting and enjoying, with experiencing and achieving, but just with love—not with being loved, but with loving.

We all want to be loved. We would all like the fulfillment that we dream of as the perfect marriage.

But Jesus taught another kind of fulfillment, the kind he sought for himself and came to symbolize: the fulfillment of crucified love.

"Whoever loses his life. . .will save it" (Luke 9:24)

Ordinarily, we think of loving those who love us. Love is a reciprocal arrangement; we give it because we receive it. Especially do we hope to be loved in marriage.

But Jesus taught us the ideal of committing ourselves without guarantee of reward; without the certainty of getting anything for ourselves except the reality of being given and the opportunity to live out our commitment in love.

What Jesus actually did was change the goal— in a sense, even the nature—of marriage. He proposed that what both parties in a marriage should aim at above all things, and set their hearts on, was not just the enjoyment of a fruitful, fulfilling life of mutual compatibility, but the total gift of self in love.

The important thing would be not what one received, but what one gave. Instead of describing

the ideal wife—as she is described, for example, in
the last chapter of the Book of Proverbs—or the
ideal husband, Jesus proposes love itself as the
ideal. And this ideal is the enduring love, the unconditional kindness and fidelity of God himself.
(See Exodus 34:6 and John 1:14.) It is the love
that Jesus himself showed when, having "loved his
own in this world," he accepted crucifixion in order to "show his love for them to the end."
(See John 13:1).

The essential thing a Christian entering marriage should hope for is not to *find* the perfect husband or wife, but to *become* the perfect image of
God through love; that is, through learning to love
as God loves. This is what Christian marriage promises as personal fulfillment. And it is this which
makes Christian marriage a path to that "perfection of charity" which Vatican II holds up as the
goal of every truly Christian life (*Constitution on
the Church*, #40).

The beautiful "Prayer of St. Francis" captures
not only the generosity and selflessness of this
ideal, but the spirit of joy that should characterize
and flow from it:

> O Divine Master,
> grant that I may not so much seek
> to be consoled
> as to console;
> to be understood
> as to understand;
> to be loved,
> as to love;
> for it is in giving
> that we receive,

       it is in pardoning
       that we are pardoned,
       and it is in dying
       that we are born to eternal life.

These are beautiful words—and a beautiful prayer for the married and unmarried alike. But we can say them or sing them over and over again without understanding them if we do not reflect on the reality that makes a prayer like this possible.

Crucified love—or love committed to accepting even continual crucifixion rather than fail in its commitment—is an intelligible ideal only if we believe that total fulfillment has already been won and given to us independently of what we might enjoy or not enjoy on this earth. It only makes sense if we believe that fulfillment comes through our choices, not through our good fortune, and especially through our choice of Jesus Christ and his choice of us.

It is this belief that frees us from worry about what we receive. It frees us to concentrate on what we can give.

To be more concerned after an argument with consoling the other's hurt than with finding consolation for our own; to keep trying to understand another with an open mind even when we ourselves are misunderstood; to continue trying to communicate our deepest thoughts and feelings after repeated misunderstandings or rejection; to seek our fulfillment in giving love rather than in receiving it without turning this into psychological withdrawal or a martyr's complex; to pardon others even when doing so feels like dying from the inside out, and to commit ourselves to doing this unconditionally

all our lives long—all this is possible and worthwhile only if we have more to hope for than just
the experience of union with another person, more
to trust in than just the visible likelihood of the
other's response, more to live for than just what we
receive from one another.

There is a myth about the power of "romantic love," as if our depth of feeling for another
could carry us through all the growth process of a
lifelong commitment. This is a myth. Feelings
come and go. They are no more reliable than the
winds of the sea. They drive us passionately, storm-
ily, gently, or leave us becalmed.

Feelings are sufficient for romantic attach-
ments, as a short breeze is enough for sailing across
a pond. But anyone crossing the ocean must reckon
with a lot of different weather. Love is a long-term
process—a process of gradual and sometimes pain-
ful growth. Feelings are not long-term.

The depth or strength of our feeling is not the
measure of our love: only our souls are the measure
of our love. And commitment is the measure of
our souls.

Our souls are the measure of our love. And
our souls are a word we speak in response to the
God who first spoke us into existence.

Only within this word of our response to God
can the words of our response to another creature
be grounded in what is completely and eternally
true, beautiful and good. It is the constancy of
God's goodness that provides the horizon for our
enduring response to the unstable goodness of one
another. Every created person or value comes
across to us now as good, now as not so good; now

as enticingly desirable, now as not even worth the effort. It is the goodness of God backing up the goodness of creatures that keeps us persevering in love until the love that we give draws forth from another the love we hoped to find.

And if we never find it in another, we have already found it in God.

The crucifixion of Jesus, then, is not only a symbol of self-giving. It is also a symbol of transcendence, of human acceptance of the call to destiny and fulfillment beyond this world.

Jesus could give up his life in this world because no one could take from him the eternal life that was already his. For us to accept the crucifixion of Jesus as the symbol of our own life is to accept fulfillment in God as our destiny. This makes us radically free with regard to any passing fulfillment on earth.

It is only on the basis of such an acceptance—on the part of both parties—that unconditional marriage makes sense.

When both husband and wife believe in the meaning and fulfillment of life as taught by Jesus, the Master of the Way, then their love can be an unconditional commitment to each other, "till death do us part."

Each will seek the fulfillment of marriage through giving. And giving is something that is always ours to do.

In a Christian marriage, then, sexual intercourse is the expression, not just of love, but of the love Jesus taught: an unconditional, total self-giving unto death.

This makes sex an expression, not just of human commitment, but of commitment through the power of God. The good news about sex is that Jesus Christ has made it the expression of a level of love that is proper to God alone.

14.

Not 'Being Good' but 'Being For'
The morality of the body of Christ

The event of Jesus Christ changed the terms
of human life on earth: Jesus changed the meaning
of fulfillment by offering the "pearl of great
price"—the Kingdom, himself—as human destiny.
He changed the meaning of *love* through his crucifixion. He changed the meaning of *marriage and
sex* by changing life and love—and in one other
way: He made our bodies his.

We have so often heard the expression "body
of Christ" used of the Church, and of ourselves,
that we may have grown used to it without understanding what it means. It is *not* just a symbolic
way of speaking (such as a metaphor, a figure of
speech). It is a carefully chosen, precise formula
of words designed to express in human language,
as clearly as possible, the truth of what we are.

Our existence—the life we feel, experience, and act by—is a mystery of the human and the divine made one. We are both human and divine.

This is so, not because human nature includes some "spark of the divine," some godlike element that is a participation in divinity. There is not, by nature, something transcendent in us that we can "get in touch with" through meditation. The only level of consciousness we can naturally reach through meditation is the ocean floor of our own souls—the quiet depths of our own human knowledge and freedom.

The fact that we have intellects and wills, that we can think and choose, that we are rational and free, just makes us *like* God; it doesn't make us divine. By nature we are created in God's image, but we do not actually participate in God's own act of existing; we don't live by God's own personal life. We live on our level; God lives on his.

But the union with God which we can have through grace is quite different. By grace—which literally means the "favor" of God's joining us to himself—we actually become divine.

Through the favor of union with God—grace—we share in God's own life as he lives it. We participate in what he does, in his own act of knowing and loving, while he is doing it. Our life is no longer just human life; it is a communication to us of God's own personal life. He comes to live within us so that we might be brought into his action as sharers in his very life. Our life is no longer just created life; it is eternal life—the uncreated life of God himself. And we live by it—on God's own level of existence.

This means we are no longer just in God's image. In us God himself lives, moves, acts, does his own personal thing. We are not just the image of God; we are the real thing. It is God himself who appears and acts in us.

We are mystery

All this may sound very confusing, but there is a difference between what is confusing and what is simply a mystery too deep to comprehend. Confusion suggests a tangle of thought and words, of ideas we have to set down and get straight. Mystery is like a well of deep water; we just cannot see to the bottom.

Our union with God is not really confusing; it is just a mystery. No matter how clear we get the expression of it in our heads, we can grow forever in understanding and appreciating it.

But the reality of Jesus Christ helps us to understand. What was Jesus? He was not just the image of God; he was God in human flesh.

Some theologians in the first years of Christianity took the expression "God in human flesh" to mean that Jesus was just God *in* a human body; that is, God was present in Jesus, but Jesus was not totally God. According to them, Christ's human body was not divine; it was just a body God used. Human flesh, they said, cannot itself be divine; so Jesus was just a divine person living and acting in a non-divine, human body. The spirit of Jesus was divine, but not his flesh.

This explanation was rejected by the Church. Scripture, the Church declared, calls Jesus the Word *made* flesh. In Jesus God *became* flesh, became a human being with a body. The body of Jesus is just as divine as Jesus is; and Jesus is divine, the eternal Son of God, equal to the Father in every way.

We are not trying here to explain *how* all this can be true. Even to understand what a human intellect can understand of this mystery we would have to go a lot more deeply into philosophy and theology than is possible here. We just want to emphasize that it is true, so that we can bring home to ourselves in some way the mystery and reality of our own existence.

We are the body of Christ; not just by the fact of existing, as Christ's own body was, but by the fact that Christ has joined us to himself (which is the favor that the word *grace* means). Our existence is now a coexistence with Christ. On the personal level—the level of *who*—he has joined himself to us in such a way that on the level of nature—of our *what*—we and Christ are able to act as one. We truly belong to him; we are part of him. In what we do he truly acts in us and we in him because we really are his body on earth.

This means that our actions are divine. They are his. And we ourselves can be called divine because we live by the divine life of Christ the way the parts of our bodies live by the life of the whole body. We are incorporated into his own flesh; we are members of the divine body of Jesus Christ.

The best way to understand this, perhaps, is to look at the union of grace when it is perfect. The human being who most clearly reveals to us the reality of graced human life is Mary, the mother of Jesus.

The life of Jesus was not "graced" as ours is. Jesus was not "full of grace" as Mary was. He was grace incarnate. His union with the Father was not a favor he received; it was his by right. Jesus is Son of God by nature. We are God's children by incorporation into Jesus. We receive grace—or the favor of union with God—by being incorporated into that union with God which is the very existence of Jesus Christ.

Mary was just a graced human being like ourselves. If we can understand the difference between Mary and Jesus, we can understand the difference between Jesus and ourselves. If we can understand the similarity between Mary and Jesus, we can understand the similarity between Jesus and ourselves. What is different, then, and what is the same, in the mystery of Mary's being and the mystery of Jesus, the Word-made-flesh?

When God wanted to become human, he had to make a choice. Human beings come in two varieties, male and female, and God couldn't be both at once. He chose to take flesh as a male.

By becoming flesh as a man, God lost all the posibilities open to him for revealing his goodness and beauty as a woman. There are just some things about the way God is that a woman's human nature can reveal more eloquently than a man's. The Greeks showed their recognition of this by worshiping both gods and goddesses. The Chinese speak of yin and yang.

God's solution to the problem was to give us Jesus and Mary.

Mary was not God. But she was "full of grace." That means that her *who* was so perfectly

united to the *who* of God—her person so completely surrendered to his—that God could do anything
in her human nature that he wanted. She put up no
resistance.

Whatever God wanted to express through
Mary's human nature as a woman he could express
without any limitations imposed by her free will.
Mary remained free, of course—but so perfectly
surrendered to God in faith and love that her humanity was totally at his disposal. In her God could
do, be and express anything her human nature was
capable of doing or expressing. And she expressed
herself with him. She made his expression her own.
She became, as a person, all that God expressed in
her. She created herself by her responses to him.

This means that Mary's human nature was as
completely surrendered to the divinity of the God
who had joined himself to her in grace as the human nature of Christ was surrendered to his own
divinity. Anything the person of Jesus could express in his own human nature as a man, God could
express in the human nature of Mary as a woman.

Mary was not God. Everyone is clear about
that. But because she was full of grace, Mary was
the perfect expression of what God would have
been as a woman.

This means that if Mary had been a feminine
incarnation of God we would not have *seen* any
difference.

What does this have to do with us?

Being male or female is not the only difference that exists between human beings. Jesus was
not just a man; he was a Jewish man, a first-century
man from a small town in the country.

Had God taken flesh as Chinese, or grown up in a big city in modern times, or been born as a retarded child, each one of these incarnations would have allowed God to show us something of his own truth, goodness and beauty that was not and could not be revealed just in the human nature of Jesus of Nazareth.

That is one reason why God has need of us.

God asks each one of us to do, essentially, what he asked Mary to do: to give our flesh to be the flesh of God. He does not ask us to become the mother of God in the way that Mary was—to conceive and give birth in the biological sense. But he asks us to let Christ be born in us in the sense St. Paul gives to these words throughout his letters to the early Christians. He asks us to give our whole bodies to be the body of Christ—to "offer our bodies as a living sacrifice" to God—so that Christ might live and act in us. He asks us "not to conform" to the attitudes and values, to the behavior of our culture, but to "be transformed by the renewal of our minds"; that is, to let ourselves be guided by Christ the way the members of a human body are directed by their head.

He asks us to be his body on earth.

When we accept grace—accept the favor of union with God that is offered to us by Jesus Christ—it is not just we who are doing something. When we give ourselves to Christ to be his body we are not just dedicating ourselves. God does something, too. He unites himself to us. He communicates to us a sharing in his own life; he comes to live his life in us and to join us to what he personally is doing. "In Christ," Paul writes, "the fullness of deity resides in bodily form." And he goes on to say, "Yours is a share of this fullness, in him. . ." (Colossians 2:9).

We really become the body of Christ, his flesh upon earth. When we act according to his inspirations, he acts in us—so much so that our actions are truly called divine. They are Christ's own actions, Christ expressing himself through us.

How does this affect our thinking about sex?

The fact that we are the body of Christ leads us to think in two directions: that of *morality*, and that of *mystery*.

Christian morality

The guiding aim of Christian morality is not being *good*; it is being *for*. Christians do not just love what is "right"; they love Jesus Christ and want to respond to him. They want to give a welcome to his words, to receive them and live by them as proof of their loyalty and friendship for Christ.

The starting point of all Christian morality, then, is a sense of belonging. We belong to Christ; we are not our own. We are given to Christ and he is given to us. We have a covenant with him. We have agreed to be his body.

People who are married seldom speak of purity. They speak of fidelity, of being faithful. For them, sexual purity is not just a matter of abstract right and wrong; it is a matter of being faithful to one another.

The Christian is a person whose basic consciousness of self is a joyful realization of being given to Christ, of belonging to him. At least, this

182

is what it should be. If, as is too often the case, we have not yet arrived at this fundamental awareness of deep, personal gift and relationship to Christ, then nothing else in Christian belief or practice can really be understood by us as it should. Certainly not Christian sexual ideals. A Christian is never just pure; he or she is always pure as an act of fidelity to Jesus Christ. Purity is not just a burden, a restrictive prohibition. It is an active response to Christ. There is joy in it.

The early Christians had a keen sense of this relationship dating from their Baptism. Many of them had been baptized as adults, and the moment remained in their memories as the turning point of their lives. They had gone down into the water as a symbol of going down into the grave with Christ, and they had come out of the water consecrated—committed to living as the risen body of Jesus on earth. The goal and focus of their lives had changed.

That is why St. Paul, writing to them and to us, can say: "Since you have been raised up in company with Christ, set your heart on. . .things above rather than on things of earth." Our destiny is not in this world. He goes on to urge: "Put to death whatever in your nature is rooted in earth: fornication, uncleanness, passion, evil desires, and that lust which is idolatry." And the reason is "because you are God's chosen ones, holy and beloved!" (Colossians 3:1-12).

He put it to the Corinthians in a slightly different way: "You must know that your body is a temple of the Holy Spirit, who is within—the Spirit you have received from God. You are not your

183

own. You have been purchased, and at a price. So glorify God in your body" (1 Corinthians 6:19-20).

This basic sense of belonging to Christ, of being loved by him, united to him as his body, sealed to him by a covenant, is our fundamental motive for being pure. We are Christ's body; we love him. Therefore we live for what he lives for, not for the excitements of this world.

But the relationship we have with Christ takes us further than that. As Christ's body we are consecrated to his mission on earth. We are "co-workers" with Christ (1 Corinthians 3:9). We "glorify God in our bodies" by living in such a way that "in our bodies the life of Jesus may also be revealed" (2 Corinthians 4:10).

What this means is that we have adopted, as Christians, a standard of morality different from that of simple right and wrong. The Christian's first question when faced with a decision should not be, "Is this okay?" but, "Can I bear witness to the values of Jesus Christ through this? Does this action reveal the life of Jesus in me, the realization I have that I am the body of Christ?"

Which one of us would want to hear from Jesus Christ some day that the way we lived for him was just okay?

"Do you love me, Lord?"

"You're okay."

"Did I help you at all on earth, Lord?"

"You did okay."

There is no good news at all in being okay— even if we are okay to God. Especially if it is God!

One thing we can thank God for all our lives is that Jesus Christ never urged anyone to be just okay. We mean more to him than that!

Yet he accepted people as okay—people who didn't really think they were and whom nobody else accepted. The lady five times divorced who was living with a man to whom she was not married (John 4:4); the crooked businessman (Luke 19:1); the quisling tax collector (Matthew 9:9). All of these found acceptance in Christ. But he didn't leave them on the level where he found them. The tax collector became one of his 12 apostles; the crooked businessman gave half of his money away to the poor; the lady with the loose sex life brought a whole town to his feet.

The great thing about Jesus is not that he *accepted* people—great as that is in itself—but that he *expected* people to be capable of such great and beautiful responses. He saw in every person something that could be called forth. And he tried to call it forth.

At some moment in our lives we become conscious, not just that we need God, but that in Jesus Christ God has said that he needs us. He needs us to be his body. He needs us to be the expression in human flesh, in our day, of all that he came to say, all that he came to do.

Jesus never tried to save the world all by himself. One of his first acts was to ask other people to help him. (See Matthew 3:18.) The essential act of redemption, the dying on the cross, was his, of course. But even to get to Calvary he needed the assistance of a passer-by named Simon who helped him carry the cross. And to bring his word and the evidence of his power and love to the world he calls us.

He calls us to give him our bodies.

When we received the sacrament of Confirmation we accepted consciously the mission of helping Jesus Christ to save the world. If that sounds presumptuous, the presumption is on God's part, not ours. He is the one who invites us!

This, too, is the meaning of the Eucharist. We offer bread and wine to God as a symbol of ourselves—as a physical, symbolic way of expressing our desire to be transformed into the body of Christ and to live now only in the way that is appropriate to his body. We commit ourselves to live by the truth and the inspirations of Christ our head, to be moved by him and to respond to him as members of his own body. We give our bodies to him so that in us and in all the members of his body on earth, he might continue to live and act and carry out his redemptive mission in human form until the end of the world.

This is the call Jesus is extending to us in that text from St. Paul that we keep citing in this book: "And now, brothers, I beg you through the mercy of God to offer your bodies as a living sacrifice. . . . Do not conform yourselves to this age. . ." (Romans 12:1-2).

To break with the patterns of our culture in the area of sexual behavior is not an easy thing to do. We have already mentioned the pressure that is on all of us—not just on youth!—to conform to the manners and morals presented to us on television, in advertisements, through sexually exploitative clothes styles, through speech patterns that are increasingly obscene, in books and conversations where casual sex between the unmarried is taken

186

for granted and "committed" sex (between the un-committed!) held up as an ideal.

Christ doesn't just ask us to resist all this. He asks us to counter it with an ideal of our own—of his own—that is based on the awareness we have of ourselves as the body of Christ. He asks us to show what we stand for.

Because we are the body of Christ, St. Paul cries out to us: "I declare and solemnly attest in the Lord that you must no longer live as the pagans do. . . . You must lay aside your former way of life and old self which deteriorates through illusion and desire, and acquire a fresh, spiritual way of think-ing" (Ephesians 4:17-23).

Our conversations should reflect the aware-ness we have of our identification with Christ: "As for lewd conduct or promiscuousness or lust of any sort, let them not even be mentioned among you; your holiness forbids this. Nor should there be any obscene, silly, or suggestive talk; all that is out of place" (Ephesians 5:3-4).

For the Christian, Christ's ideals are not re-strictive; they are directive. They do not hold us back; they send us out with a joyful vision of truth to share with the world. They do not make us de-fensive—and certainly not offensive!—but they do make us different and very willing to be affirma-tive about that fact. We do not want to conform to this age. We want to be "transformed by the renewal of our minds."

We claim the right to live by a different vision; to judge by the word of Christ and the Spirit that is within us "what is God's will, what is good, pleasing and perfect."

That is Christian morality in a nutshell: to
try to do God's will—not just what is good as opposed to evil, but what is pleasing to Jesus Christ.
Better still, Christian morality is to let him do what
he wants to do in us as in his own body, for that
will be what is perfect.

In the measure we succeed in doing this—and
it is a growing process—our lives will be a source of
joy not only to ourselves, but to all who are able
to accept and to rejoice in what is good. Christ will
live in us. And Christ is the joy of the world.

The commitment to become Christ

There is more to the Christian life than this,
however. The Christian life is more than just belonging to Christ; more than just bearing witness
to him; more than simply helping Christ to fulfill
his redemptive mission on earth. The Christian life
is a form of spousal consecration to Christ.

We have said that the reality of spousal love is
a commitment to do all those things which, of
themselves, tend to lead two persons to perfect
union of mind and will and heart.

The commitment we made to Christ at Baptism, the substance of our covenant with him, is a
commitment to growing union with Christ.

St. Paul wrote to the Church in Corinth: "I
am jealous of you with the jealousy of God himself, since I have given you in marriage to one husband, presenting you as a chaste virgin to Christ."
He uses the reality of marriage to speak of our
relationship with Christ. And because we are committed to Christ in this way, Paul's one desire is
that we will attain to perfect union of mind and

heart with Christ. His one fear is that we won't: "My fear is that. . .your thoughts may be corrupted and you may fall away from your sincere and complete devotion to Christ" (2 Corinthians 11:2-3).

Those who are pledged to love one another are faithful on the level of thought before all else. The attitude they choose to take toward each other, and toward everything else, will build up or tear down their love.

Our commitment to Christ, then, is first of all on the level of thought. Our commitment is to study the mind of Christ, to discover his attitudes and values, to keep our thoughts and desires constantly in harmony with his. It is this that makes us grow in union with him.

We grow especially in those moments of temptation when we are so drawn toward other things that any harmony between ourselves and Christ seems to be nothing but free choice and the power of his grace; in other words, nothing but commitment! It is not the thoughts which come to us that make us unfaithful to Christ; it is those we allow to remain.

Joy is an essential part of this commitment. Not felt joy always, but a determination to rejoice. If Christ is a burden to us, we are hardly a credit to him! In our relationship with Christ, as in our relationship with anyone we love, our testimony to his value is our joy.

St. Paul tells us that joy can be a chosen frame of mind, so long as we have something real to rejoice in. And Christ is real. "Rejoice in the Lord always! I say it again. Rejoice!. . .The Lord is near. Dismiss all anxiety from your minds"

(Philippians 4:4-5). We have nothing to fear, nothing to worry about. Our fulfillment has been given to us; we have only to enter into the joy of it step by step.

We begin by directing our thoughts. We can hear Jesus himself speaking to us in the exhortation of St. Paul: "Finally, my brothers, your thoughts should be wholly directed to all that is true, all that deserves respect, all that is honest, pure, admirable, decent, virtuous, or worthy of praise. Live according to what you have learned and accepted, what you have heard me say and seen me do. Then will the God of peace be with you!" (Philippians 4:8-9).

The commitment is not just on our side, however. Christ, too, is committed to making us one with himself: to sharing his mind and heart with us, to purifying us and filling us with life. Paul describes Christ as preparing his Church—that is, us— the way a bridegroom prepares his bride for complete and total union with himself: "He gave himself up for her to make her holy, purifying her in the bath of water by the power of the word, to present to himself a glorious church, holy and immaculate, without stain or wrinkle or anything of that sort" (Ephesians 5:25-27).

Since we have this commitment from Christ, and all the promises God has made to us, St. Paul encourages us to take heart and work with joy to "purify ourselves from every defilement of flesh and spirit, and. . .strive to fulfill our consecration perfectly" (2 Corinthians 7:1).

That is what the Christian ideal in sex is all about. It is not just refraining from evil; it is total

consecration to Christ in all we do, total fidelity
to him to whom before all others we belong. It is a
way to grow toward perfect union with him.

15.

The Dimension Jesus Added
The mystery of sacramental sex

What Christians understand as morality is already response to mystery. A Christian choice is never just a decision between right and wrong; it is a response to the mystery of God's love for us.

Everything we do as Christians should express the mystery of our belonging to Christ as his body. Yet when the focus is on morality as such, this mystery tends to stay in the background. In the last chapter we centered our attention on the way we *should* act *because* we are the body of Christ: This is morality. Now we want to center on the way we *can* act *as* the body of Christ: This is more specifically mystery.

In this chapter we want to focus specifically on the mystery of what it means to express ourselves sexually as the body of Christ.

Let's first approach it through an example that has nothing to do with sex: Walking down the hall one day, I see someone coming who is really depressed. Suppose God speaks to me in my heart and says, "Let's smile at that person."

This may not come across to me as an inspiration of grace or a message from on high. It may never occur to me that God has anything to do with it. I just get the thought of smiling. It is a loving impulse. Already this thought and this impulse are mine as well as God's. God and I together are having one thought: "Let's smile at that person." Together we desire to do it.

Suppose I don't follow through. Suppose I remember that I smiled at that same person the day before and got snubbed for my kindness, really put down. I could refuse to smile. In that case I just walk on, and the graced act never happens.

But suppose I do smile. (This is what Jesus meant when he said we should turn the other cheek: not withdrawing when we are rejected; sticking our necks out again and again in order to keep in relationship with other people.) If I smile, that smile is literally both human and divine. It is a graced smile. The person I smile at is being smiled at by God.

If I smile, it is God himself who is smiling; God is smiling in me. I am his body; it is his smile. He is doing it with me.

At the same time, I am expressing through my smile an infinite, divine act of love. And it is *my* act of love. Because God has united me to himself as his own body, his act of love is my own.

This is what a graced action is: It is one and

the same action which is both God's personal act and a human personal act, while remaining one single action. There are not two acts of love, human and divine, that blend. Nor is God doing the loving while I do the smiling. There is just one act of love expressed in one smile, and the reality of this loving smile is both human and divine. God and I each share completely in what the other does.

This is what sexual love is between Christians: one act of love, both human and divine, made flesh.

God speaks through sex

The awesome thing about Christian sexual expression is that God is expressing himself in everything we do. But if this awe inhibits us, makes sex solemn, then we haven't understood how human God becomes in us.

In the playfulness, the teasing, the sexiness of sex, God is expressing himself. The physical expression of love between Christian couples is hilarious and holy, sexy and sacred, playful and sacramental all at the same time. Whether sex is awesome and profound or teasing and light, every sexual encounter between Christian married couples is a mystery both human and divine.

If the only love expressed in sex were the love of two human beings for one another, sex would still be one of the most precious and sublime of human actions. But Christian couples are able to do more than that. They can mediate and express to one another through their physical gestures in sex the love that God himself has for them both. God makes their expressions of love to one another his own; what they say to each other in sex God says.

God gives to each partner in a marriage the power to speak for him. This is a priestly power, like that of the priest at the altar who can speak in the name of Christ when he says over bread and wine, "This is my body; this is my blood." In every gesture and word through which married couples say to one another, "You are precious to me; you are beautiful and loved; you are my delight," God is speaking.

It is not that we have to be married in order for God to express his love to another through us. But we have to be married in order to express love to another with that depth of meaning and intensity of passion which sexual gestures convey. What God gives to each member of a marriage is the power to speak for him in this way.

Sexual intercourse, for the Christian, is a sacred act from beginning to end. It is an act that involves the passionate self-offering and commitment, not only of two human persons, but of Jesus Christ as well. It is a physical, symbolic echo of the words that Jesus spoke in his passion and continues to speak through the Eucharist, words that each member of a marriage makes his or her own and that Jesus is speaking in each one: "This is my body, which is given up for you."

It is an awesome thing to be able to express to another in this way the depth of the passion and love of God. This is the mystery of sex. It is the dimension Jesus added.

This is why Christian marriage is a sacrament.

A sacrament is a visible sign instituted by

Jesus Christ to give grace; that is, to give the favor of increased union with himself.

Christian marriage is a visible sign of Christ's activity, because the two people who enter into marriage with each other are the body of Christ. They act visibly, and in them Christ is acting.

All of the words, the gestures, the symbols of the marriage ceremony—and of the couple's whole life together as husband and wife—are signs through which Jesus Christ is expressing himself.

When a couple commit their love to each other in marriage, Jesus is speaking in them—not in the sense that Jesus is committing his love *at the same time*, alongside of them, as it were, as if he were saying, "Me, too." It is rather that in the bride and bridegroom themselves Jesus is speaking. The love that the groom himself commits—his own love—is also the love of Jesus Christ. Jesus isn't saying, "I love you too"; He is saying, "In this love that he is committing he and I are one." And the same is true of the bride. There is only one love committed by each party to a marriage; and it is the divine and human love of two people who are speaking to each other as members of the body of Christ.

When Jesus shares in the promise of the wedding pair to share their whole hearts and minds with one another, Jesus is not promising to share the heart and mind he shared with us through the Gospel—his own heart and mind as such. What he is promising to share is his heart and mind precisely as it is communicated, received and understood by each of the parties to the marriage. Jesus is promising to share everything of himself that is *in them*.

197

Whenever a married couple share with each other the knowledge of Christ that is within them, they are giving to each other, and Christ is giving through them, the favor—the grace—of increased union of mind and heart with Jesus Christ. That is why it is so important for Christian couples to share the deepest levels of their spiritual lives with one another. They are committed to sharing Christ with one another by sharing their whole selves—including their deepest experience of God.

This, in part at least, is the sacramental grace of marriage. God gives grace, or the favor of increased union with himself, in many ways. He inspires our minds and moves our hearts directly, for example, through his eloquent, silent Spirit acting invisibly within us. But when God draws people to union with himself through Jesus Christ acting in a visible way through his body, this is the grace most specific to Christianity. This is the special favor of God visibly interacting with us in a human way, through the visible body of his Son.

In a sense, all grace that comes through the Church, the visible body of Christ on earth, is sacramental grace. The Church herself is the sacrament of all sacraments, the universal sacrament, the visible sign instituted by Christ to give grace which includes in itself all the other signs.

But there are seven special ways—specific, constant, identifiable ways—in which Christ promised to act through his Church in order to give and increase our union with him. These are the seven sacraments: Baptism, through which Christ gives us life; Eucharist, through which he nourishes the life he has given us; Confirmation, through which he brings it to maturity; Reconciliation, through which he restores life diminished or lost by sin; Matrimony and Holy Orders, through which he empowers us to assure the continuance of his life upon earth in individuals and in the Christian community; and the Sacrament of the Sick, through which he heals and strengthens us.

When Jesus gives the favor of increased union with himself by acting through one of the signs we call a sacrament, the union with God that comes to us in this way is called sacramental grace. The sacramental grace of marriage, then, is whatever favor of increased union with God husband and wife are able to transmit to one another by sharing themselves with each other in marriage as the body of Christ.

Intercourse as sacrament

Obviously, sexual intercourse is one of the most powerful of the sacramental signs of marriage. In intercourse Christ is saying to both man and woman whatever each is saying to the other. And he is saying it with all the passion and intensity that intercourse involves. Sexual intercourse within the sacrament of marriage is a visible sign instituted by Christ to give grace. The favor of union which it immediately brings about is union between the two persons. But since within each one is a depth of knowledge and love of God—a goodness that is the life of God within each one—when they communicate themselves to one another they are communicating God.

It should, then, be clear that even if sexual relations outside of marriage were not against morality in general, they would still be a denial of the Christian mystery. In the Christian understanding of sex, two people are giving themselves to one another as all that they are. And all that they are includes the mystery of their being as the body of Christ.

If we are the body of Christ, if we are "not our own" as St. Paul says, but have given our bodies to Christ in Baptism, then obviously we cannot give our bodies to another unless Jesus is a party to the agreement.

That is why Christian marriage is not really complete unless in the act of forming the covenant Jesus speaks his word. Jesus must say, along with the bride and groom in the marriage ceremony, "This is my body, which is given up for you."

It is also the mystery of Christian marriage which explains, ultimately, why marriage can be forever. A man and woman can give themselves unconditionally, irrevocably to one another because their commitment rests not just on their own strength but on the strength and fidelity of Jesus Christ who commits himself in each. The love that we count on in marriage is the enduring love of God himself.

That is why St. Paul teaches that the union between husband and wife in marriage is an image, a visible representation here on earth, of the union that exists between Christ and his Church. Husband and wife can no more abandon or reject one another than Christ will abandon or reject his Church.

If a Christian couple live together in such a way that Christ is truly part of their marriage, then

Christ's own strength becomes theirs. This doesn't happen by some one-sided gift of God, as if by magic. Rather, when two people sincerely try to base their lifestyle, their choices, the decisions they make together on the teachings of Christ, they will learn the attitudes, values and behavior that strengthen love rather than diminish it. St. John tells us "God is love" (1 John 4:16). God knows a lot about it!

If a couple pray together, take time to read and reflect on God's word together, to discuss its meaning and its application to their lives, then Christ will be able to speak to them through his word, and speak to them through each other. He will be able to give them life through his word—to guide, strengthen, console, encourage, enlighten and fill them with trust. He will lead them through his word to a way of living together that is satisfying, joyful and constantly opening to deeper and deeper experience of each other. He will be the mind of their marriage, the heart and soul of each one's commitment, creativity and love.

Sex between people who have a relationship on this level is really good news.

Part III:
Being the Good News
to One Another

What we do follows from what we are. What we choose to do expresses the understanding we have of ourselves, the value we place on ourselves. Our sexual behavior, therefore, when it is free and deliberate, expresses both the understanding we have of ourselves as human beings and the meaning and value we attach to our sexuality as such.

In Part I we reflected on our humanity. We saw that, in order to live the full reality of human life, we must accept ourselves as *created* for a purpose, as *creating ourselves* by choices, and as *called* to the destiny of sharing in the life of God as the body of Christ on earth. Not to live on all the levels of human life simultaneously—the physical, cultural, personal and graced—is to live a diminished human existence.

In Part II we saw how all these levels of human life must be present in our sexual activity in order for sexual behavior to be authentic. In the measure that any level of human life and existence is missing from our sexual activity, in that same measure we are denying our sexuality. Any sexual behavior, therefore, that is not physically, culturally, personally and spiritually authentic strips sex of some of its meaning and value. It is sex diminished or distorted in some way, sex that "misses."

But the basic meaning of sin is "that which misses." The ordinary word for sin in the New Testament is the Greek word *hamartia:* that which misses the mark, falls short of being what it ought to be.

In Part III, therefore, we want to bring into focus some guidelines for behavior that will help us keep our sexuality intact—keep it whole, unfragmented and undiminished—and keep ourselves together as human beings. Our target value will be wholeness. And our guiding principle will be that human sexual activity, in order to be fully authentic, must be physically expressive, culturally responsible, personally sincere and spiritually graced. In the measure that we express the wholeness of human life and sexuality this way, we become the "good news" about life and about sex to one another.

16.

When Is Touching Sexual?
A look at touch on four levels

One thing too many people seem to want to avoid these days is answering concrete questions on just what is right and wrong in the area of sexual activity before marriage.

Joyce Maynard, whom we quoted earlier, said it writing for *Newsweek* when she was 19: "The big line I remember from our school days was, 'There is no right answer. What's your *opinion*?' "

No one wants to be dogmatic. So true is this that one almost begins to feel that the most dogmatic proclamation being made in the area of sexual morality today is the untouchable assumption that there are no absolute prohibitions! It seems to be the first article of a counselor's creed—or perhaps an unadmitted loyalty test—to begin any discussion of sex by agreeing that no concrete act of physical intimacy between consenting adults can be ruled out as always and intrinsically wrong, whether in or outside of marriage.

For those who take this position the relevant questions are not about right and wrong, but about what is wise or unwise, adult or immature, self-integrating or destructive for the persons involved. The young are cautioned to ask themselves whether they are sufficiently mature to deal with an intimate physical relationship. Or they are urged to consult their feelings and see if they are really being true to themselves.

The focus is not on whether a particular kind of behavior is right or wrong, but just on whether you can handle it. What will the behavior do to you emotionally, now or later? How will it affect the quality of your relationship with your partner? What effect might it have on your ability to respond sexually in marriage later on?

All of these questions are important, of course. I could fill chapters with conclusions from psychologists, statistics from sociologists and observations from experienced counselors and experts in the area of sex, all pointing out the dangers of premarital petting and intercourse. The overwhelming consensus of the experts seems to be that sex before marriage is bad news. They just differ on the degree of physical intimacy they consider dangerous, and on how universally dangerous they consider it to be.

But I left those chapters out. In the back of my mind kept ringing a passage from Thomas Merton's autobiography, *The Seven Storey Mountain* (Harcourt, Brace and Co., 1948), in which he described a chaplain at his English boys' school who based all of Christian morality on the value of being a gentleman. As Merton remembers him:

> There he stood, in the plain pulpit, and raised his chin above the heads of all the rows of boys in black coats, and said: "One might go through this chapter of St. Paul [1 Corinthians 13] and simply substitute the word 'gentleman' for 'charity' wherever it occurs. 'If I talk with the tongues of men and angels, and be not a gentleman, I am become as sounding brass, or a tinkling cymbal. . . . A gentleman is patient, is kind; a gentleman envieth not, dealeth not perversely; is not puffed up. . . . A gentleman never falleth away. . . .' "
>
> And so it went. I will not accuse him of finishing the chapter with "Now there remain faith, hope and gentlemanliness, and the greatest of these is gentlemanliness. . . ," although it was the logical term of his reasoning.

No one is particularly turned on by the idea of being a gentleman these days—or a lady. But we would be making essentially the same mistake as Merton's mannerly chaplain if we built our moral teaching on the foundation of any human value—no matter how relevant—instead of on the simple absolute of loving an all-lovable God.

Sexual purity is an imperative—ultimately not because impurity is disintegrating to the personality, or hurts others, or endangers our chances of having a happy marriage later on, or is a violation of our personal word, true as I believe all these

207

arguments to be. Purity is something we are impelled to, in the last analysis, not for any human reason but simply because in the depths of our hearts as creatures we know this to be something required of us by the wisdom and will of God.

I have tried, in all of the preceding chapters, to present an argument for sexual purity based on the meaning and value of sexual expression itself. It would be a mistake, however, to stop with the value of sex as if it were an ultimate. Of course it is important to respect the value of sex as such. But that importance rests on the fact that sex is created by God. The inescapable truth is that any position we take toward sex in our lives is at the same time a position we take toward God.

Sexual purity is a value like truth, or justice, or love, or respect for human life. It is a value in itself, which must be respected for what it is in itself. Not to do so is a failure in respect for God.

Whenever we attempt to give to sexual expression a meaning that fits our fancy instead of the meaning sex has in itself from God, we are doing two things: We are trying to recreate sex in our own image; and, we are refusing our own reality as created in the image of God. We are presuming to be not creatures but the Creator. We are acting not as graced, rational beings able to express in our behavior the wisdom and beauty of God, but as something else of our own making. And this is the original sin of pride: By excluding God's intention and purpose in the use of any of our powers, sexual or otherwise, we are declaring ourselves independent of God. We are refusing not just to love him, but even to recognize who he is.

When we deny who God is for us, however, we are at the same time involving ourselves in the most radical denial of who we are. We are placing all of human life on a false basis. Almost anything can follow from that.

If sex has meaning and value in itself which we as intelligent beings created in the image of God are able to discover, then by using sex according to its true meaning and value we will enter into all the enrichment of life which sex is able to provide. The more we understand and experience everything God has enabled sex to be for us, the more we will appreciate the good news about sex.

On the other hand, if we do not respect the meaning and value that sex has, we sin not only against the value of sex itself, but against our own relationship with God.

We have already seen that sex has overlapping value on all four levels of human life. In a vastly simplified form, we can give an indication of the value of sex on each level as follows:

1) On the physical level, the value of sex is to give life. This value is appropriate only within the context of a stable marriage, which provides children with a family to grow up in.

2) On the cultural level, the way we express ourselves as sexual beings is a way of building up or tearing down our own and others' appreciation of what sex is and of how people should relate to one another as men and women. On this level sex presents us with an opportunity and a challenge to use our masculinity or femininity in constructive, creative ways for one another.

3) On the personal level, sex is the expression

of spousal love. Love, we have seen, means commitment. And the particular kind of commitment sex expresses is the commitment which married people make to one another: the total and permanent gift of self. Therefore, sex outside of the actual commitment of marriage is either a lie or a denial of the essential meaning and value of sexual expression itself.

4) On the transcendent or graced level, sex is the expression of Christ and a human person acting as one. It is an action both human and divine, an expression of love and commitment between two members of the body of Christ, each of whom has the power to speak to the other through the physical gestures of sex in the name of Jesus himself. As an expression which involves the person of Christ, sex presupposes the union of the two spouses in a sacramental marriage.

These values correspond to the *what, who* and *why* of human existence; to our *nature, person* and *destiny* as beings who are *created*, who *create ourselves* by choices, and who are *called* to the favor of union with God which is grace.

Everything we have seen so far about the meaning and value of sex leads us to the same conclusion: Truly sexual expression simply has no place at all outside of the committed relationship of marriage. All truly sexual expression outside of marriage is a denial of the authentic meaning and value of sex.

Not 'how far' but 'when to begin'

It isn't a matter of asking "how far" one can go before marriage in giving sexual expression to one's affection for another. If sex is the language of committed, married love, then sex should be reserved entirely for marriage. The language should be kept pure and authentic.

To use a language to say something you don't really mean—or don't mean yet, although you intend to mean it some day—and then to ask, "Well, how strongly can I say this before I actually mean it?" is absurd. Either our words—including our sexual words—mean what they say or they don't. To mean "a little bit" of what we say is to be "a little bit" truthful, which is the most deceptive form of lie.

Is it possible to be more or less committed? Not really. Whenever we use words this way, we are not thinking of what the words mean. Commitment is the same as gift. We can be more or less decided to give somebody something, but as long as we are more or less decided the gift is not a fact. Once something is given, however, there is no more or less about it. To speak of something as being "more or less" given is absurd. It is precisely the finality that makes the difference between a gift and a loan.

We can commit more or less of ourselves to another. We can be committed for a longer or shorter time, or subject to certain conditions. But the commitment itself either is a fact or it isn't. And none of these qualifications apply to sex.

The commitment sex expresses is the commitment of spousal love, which by definition is both total and permanent. The very language of sex expresses the removal of all barriers to the total gift and possession of the body and of the person.

211

Just as sexual arousal by its very nature prepares the body for intercourse, and tends to leave a person unsatisfied and frustrated if not carried to its logical conclusion, so all truly sexual gestures are a natural expression of the commitment to seek total union of mind and will and heart with another person. And if they don't lead to this union there is a realization that something promised has not been attained. As such, sexual intimacies are meaningless outside of a lifelong commitment. Total union with another person includes union with all that person is and will become. There is no short-term commitment to oneness.

There is no way, then, that two people can authentically use sex, or any truly sexual action, to express a partial gift of self, or commitment to a temporary relationship, or a decision not yet fully made to belong someday to each other provided nothing intervenes in the meantime to change the mind of either party. Sex either means what it says or it doesn't.

If sex is the language of spousal commitment, let's not ask ourselves where it should stop, or how far it should go, but when it should begin. All truly sexual expressions are inauthentic for Christians, therefore, if they do not include:

• the value of being a family open to giving new life;

• the value of contributing in a positive way to what it means to be a man or a woman;

• the value of expressing committed, spousal love;

• the value of mediating the love of Christ to one another.

Now the question we must answer is: What specific physical gestures are truly sexual? When does a word that we speak in our flesh cease to be just a word of closeness or affection and become a word of sexual expression, a word that is the symbol of our total gift of self?

In our culture we tend to be all mixed up about this. There are some healthy signs of change, but by and large we still tend to associate all close, affectionate touching with sex. This leads us, before we are married, sometimes to use sex just for the sake of touching; and, after we are married, to use touching just for the sake of sex. In our confusion we botch things both ways.

A mix-up about touching

Long before little children in our society are aware of sexual attraction, they absorb from the adult world the idea that touching the human body is suspect if not indecent. They are constantly told not to touch, and adults set the example. Many parents are hesitant to touch their children, or perhaps so unconsciously inhibited that they just don't think about it at all.

As Dr. Sidney Simon explains it, they "were not touched by their families, and so they don't touch their own children, who will not touch their own children, and so on" ("Please Touch," *Scholastic Teacher*, October, 1974). These parents deny to their children what Dr. William Masters and Virginia Johnson call the "spontaneous physical expression of feelings—the stroking, snuggling and enfolding movements with which almost all living creatures seek. . .warmth and reassurance" ("Touching—And Being Touched," *Redbook*, October, 1972). They are thereby training their children to restrain all impulse to reach out frankly and openly to other human beings in their desire for physical contact.

They reach out in other ways. "You can see them in any junior high school," Dr. Simon says. "They are the ones who shove and push. They knock one another down the stairwell and slam the locker door on each other's head. And behind every push and shove, they are crying out their. . . needs."

When these same kids reach adolescence they turn to sexual touching—to kissing, necking and petting, sometimes even to intercourse—not really knowing always whether what they want is sex or just a feeling of physical closeness and caring from another human being. Or else they go to the opposite extreme and avoid all affectionate touching out of fear that it may be sexual.

Most of us do both: We avoid the innocent, nonsexual expressions of affection without recognizing how inhibited we are by a guilt we should not feel. And at the same time, we satisfy our needs through touching that really is sexual while trying to rationalize the guilt we *should* feel about that!

Our sexual touching during adolescence just helps confuse us more. We are confirmed in the association we have already been conditioned to make between touching and sexual advances. Reaching out physically to another, say Masters and Johnson, "is now stripped of all significance except that of sexual provocation. Thus the use of touch as a natural, uncomplicated way to express goodwill or friendship is forfeited."

Girls learn through experience that if they allow the expression of affection to become physical at all, boys are liable to interpret this as sexual willingness and push things to a point they find embarrassing to handle.

Boys, too, are victims of our society's confusion between affectionate touching and sex. Our society makes little or no provision for legitimate touching outside of sexual relationships. What in itself might be just a desire for physical closeness, intimacy and warmth, therefore, a boy is set up to interpret as desire for sexual experience. And since sexual desire is never completely absent, the young man lumps all of his desires together indiscriminately and seeks to satisfy them all through sex. Usually the results are disappointing. In this mixup of motives, ends and means, with an admixture of guilt to add to the confusion, neither touching nor sex can do what either is supposed to.

Part of the answer is to restore to nonsexual touching its authentic place in human relationships. Masters and Johnson point out what a boon this would be to marriage. When touch is exclusively identified as sexual invitation or technique, its value is lost as a language. And then even sexual touching is impoverished. An authentic use of touch throughout a married couple's daily life together puts their sexual encounters into the proper context of mutual understanding and love.

Among the unmarried, if simple, affectionate physical contact were taken for granted and not rendered suspect by the bugaboo of sex, Dr. Simon wonders, "how much less grief and anxiety and deep feelings of inadequacy we would find in our young people. How much less jumping into bed with the first person who strokes them gently."

This is easier said than done, of course. We should not minimize the difficulty, or the danger of rationalization, or even the very real possibility that affectionate touching might ignite into passionate embracing and carry a couple farther than either had intended.

Dr. Simon is speaking to married couples when he writes: "Admittedly, the line is a very fine one and sexuality can spill over almost instantly. But all of us have given our own children back rubs and tousled their hair and kissed them all over when they were babies. We have given body comfort to friends who have fallen and hurt themselves. We have held people in our arms while they cried in grief over the loss of a loved one. We have done all that and have also touched for sexual arousal. We know the difference."

Can it be said that married couples are capable of knowing this difference while the unmarried young are not? Dr. Simon doesn't think so. Nor do I. I believe that, married or unmarried, striving for normalcy in touch is the safest course we can pursue. We have to learn to be affectionate in honest, spontaneous ways—ways that are physical without being sexual, intimate but not erotic.

We will rationalize, no doubt. And sometimes, perhaps, we will succumb to sexual desire and "miss the mark." But the danger of sin can be minimized, and its guilt quickly taken away, if we are clear about the ideals we are trying to maintain and honest about admitting it when we fail.

Guidelines on what is sexual

We need, however, some clear guidelines on what makes an action sexual. The guidelines are not all that difficult to establish.

As human beings we act on four levels simultaneously: the physical, the cultural, the personal and the graced or transcendent:

1) On the physical level an act can be sexual in itself.

2) On the cultural level an act can be sexual in one culture and not sexual in another.

3) On the personal level our intention can make almost any action sexual, whether it is in itself or not.

4) And on the transcendent level our union with God in grace has nothing to do with whether an action is sexual or nonsexual; it simply makes our legitimate human expression divine, whatever the nature of the act itself might be.

Let us explore this in detail.

Physically, any action is sexual which, given the facts of human biology, either tends by its very nature to produce orgasm (such as sexual intercourse or masturbation) or which could not reasonably be engaged in by any normal person without the intention of producing or experiencing sexual arousal (prolonged heavy kissing, for example).

Culturally, any action is sexual which, within one's own culture, would normally and legitimately be taken as a sign of sexual intimacy. Such actions would ordinarily tend to be sexually arousing for the members of the culture. In American cul-

217

ture nakedness between the sexes would normally be an act of sexual intimacy, as would any touching or feeling of the sexual organs or more private parts of the body.

Obviously, circumstances have a lot to do with whether or not an action in this category would be sexual or not. The same action might be totally nonsexual in a doctor's office as part of a physical examination, and extremely sexual in a bedroom as a way of responding to one's date.

It is in the area of actions which are normally considered sexual in the culture—and which are normally sexually arousing to members of the culture—that it is difficult to lay down absolute rules. One person might be able to do something in one particular set of circumstances which another person could not—and which he himself could not do in a different set of circumstances. I will try to offer some clearer guidelines for this category of actions in the next two chapters.

On the personal level, almost any action can be sexual if a person engages in it with the intention of seeking sexual pleasure or arousal through it. If this is what a person is really looking for, even reading certain stories from the Bible could be a sexual action!

On the other hand, if an action is not sexual in itself, and one is not engaging in it for the purpose of being sexually aroused, then even if arousal should spontaneously happen, there is no reason to call the action sexual. Sometimes sexual arousal takes place quite spontaneously and unsought, just through the normal contact of something like dancing, for example. In such cases there is no reason to feel guilty or to stop.

We should note, however, that if an action is sexual in itself, it cannot become nonsexual just through the intention of the person engaging in it. Intercourse would hardly become nonsexual, for example, just because two people are engaging in it for the purpose of scientific research! In the case of objectively sexual actions, the only choice a person has is to engage in them authentically according to their true meaning and value (which means in marriage only) or to deny their meaning and value, which is to sin against the authenticity of sex.

On the transcendent level, the reality or degree of one's union with God has not the slightest effect on whether an action is sexual or non-sexual. The most we can say here is that, if an action is not objectively sexual in itself, but could easily be exploited for sexual gratification, a high degree of union with God in grace might make it possible for one person to engage in this action with a sincerely pure intention while another person might not. Usually, however, the more spiritual a person is, the less likely he or she is to presume on such a possibility.

What rules of conduct follow from all this?

17.

Clarity of Purpose and Expression
*What we shouldn't look for; what we
should express (physical-cultural guidelines)*

The first value a Christian maintains in sex is
the connection between sexual pleasure and the
commitment to giving new life.

This does not mean that we never seek any
pleasure which comes from contact with a person
of the opposite sex. The very sound of a woman's
voice is pleasant to a man, and vice versa. There is
something nice, and not necessarily sexual at all,
about holding and being held by another person,
especially of the opposite sex. The cultural differences between men and women in our society,
those traits we call masculine and feminine, make
the company of each especially delightful and
pleasing to the other. And even on the personal
and spiritual levels, men and women so often have
such different approaches to the reality both of

this world and of God that they find special enrichment in talking deeply to one another.

All of these pleasures can be called sexual in
the sense that the sex of those with whom we have
them has something to do with our enjoyment.
But they are not sexual pleasure in the way we use
the word. Some people talk of venereal or genital
pleasure instead of sexual pleasure, but I frankly
don't find that this contributes very much to clar-
ity. I think most of us know quite well when our
interest or our intention is sexual, and that is the
word we use for it. When we realize that what we
are really looking for is sexual stimulation, then,
whatever we are doing, it is time to stop.

For a male the physical movement toward
erection is one of the first signals of anticipated
sexual pleasure. It is not a certain or sufficient sign
of a sexual intention however. An erection can
take place for many reasons, even in the midst of
activities that have nothing to do with sex. The
erection is just a warning to check into one's motivation and be on guard; it is not the deciding factor
in our judgment.

Nor is the absence of erection any guarantee
of a pure intention: Someone heading for a pornographic movie, for example, with a deliberate and
conscious sexual intention does not necessarily experience an erection on the way.

In judging our motives and intentions, therefore, we cannot substitute any physical reaction
for the sincerity of our own hearts.

The physical signs of arousal in a girl are not
as obvious, but girls know when they are beginning
to get "turned on." With or without any physical

arousal, however, girls often sense that a sexual overtone has crept into whatever is happening between their partners and themselves. It is frequently vague and undefinable, but they know it is there.

Girls should insist on the right to pull back from physical contact without explanation whenever they feel uncomfortable with it. In fact, the same rule applies to contact that is not physical at all. People can sense that a situation is turning sexual, or that another person's intentions are becoming sexually oriented, long before they can identify the precise signs that reveal this to them. When a girl senses this she has the right—and, I would say, the obligation—to follow her instinctive reaction to the situation without letting herself be pressured into having to defend it. Once a boy starts asking why, the girl is on losing ground—not because she is any less equipped to debate than he is, but because she has accepted as a starting point the completely false assumption that she is not justified in following her own reactions unless she can explain them to him.

Christians accept the fact that all truly sexual pleasure is a gift which only the married have the right to seek, to give, or to receive. For that reason we refuse in the name of sexuality itself to use or be used by another person for the sake of sexual stimulation outside of marriage.

The second value that Christians are aware of in the area of sexual expression is the mutual concern that members of the human race should have for one another. There are no totally isolated individuals on this planet; everything we do affects other people, for better or for worse. Consequently we are very much aware that all of our sexual expression—not only our specifically sexual behavior, but all our ways of speaking, of dressing, of relating to members of the opposite sex, our body language, jokes and topics of conversation, the attitudes and values we express or do not express—all of these have an influence on the way other people think and feel about sex.

Often we express attitudes about sex that we don't really feel or believe. We do this in joking ways, or in casual conversation sometimes, just for the sake of fitting into the mood or tone that others have established. We don't realize, perhaps, how much the expression of an attitude toward sex, even in joking, affects other people—and how much the mere expression of an attitude tends to make that attitude our own.

My father once quit his job with a company whose ideals he did not believe in. When I asked him about it years later his only explanation was, "You become what you accept."

The same is true in the area of sexual attitudes and values: You become what you accept; and you become even more what you express.

Therefore, I would like to hold up a banner here for two ideals nobody talks about very much anymore, perhaps because they seem so unimportant. I think a more probable reason why we don't talk about them is that we are afraid to appear ridiculous. I am talking about modesty and clean speech.

Modesty

I have spent some time in Africa where in one

tribe the women wore nothing at all except a string around their waists. And there was nothing attached to the string! That is where I learned that nakedness is not pornographic. There is nothing in the human body that is pornographic.

What finally came home to me was the basic meaning of modesty. Modesty has very little to do with how much of the body you expose. Modesty is a matter of what your clothes express.

An African woman naked on a beach is not immodest. Her body is the body God gave her, and she is not conscious of displaying any part of it more than any other. But any woman dressed in clothes that are specifically designed to present her to male eyes as a sex object is immodest, whether she is conscious of it or not. And her immodesty will have its effect—with or without any conscious intention on her part—not only on others but on herself. We become what we accept, and we unconsciously incline to play the part we dress for.

When it comes to American clothes styles, I personally favor a revolution. Without meaning to include every style or designer in some sweeping accusation, I think it is commonly recognized today that the overall effect of the styles we see around us is to make sex objects out of women— and men, too.

The natural curves of the body are beautiful. There is nothing about the body as God made it which reduces it to a sex object. Look at the classical nude statues of Greek art, for example. But those same curves with cloth stretched tightly over them become a living invitation to touch. This is the psychological effect which the tight clothes styles of our culture have—especially on men. It is a teasing effect, an incentive to touch or feel. No man living can look at a woman whose blouse is tightly buttoned across her breasts, for example, without wanting to unbutton her. And the clothes designers know this very well. They design clothes for women to put on so that men will want to take them off.

The peek-a-boo effect is much the same. No man can look at a woman whose breasts are partly covered but enticingly revealed without wanting to see the rest of them. A breast completely revealed is beautiful; it is a natural part of woman and speaks of her function as a mother. But a breast without nipples is nothing but a sexual attraction, a curve that ends in empty invitation. And this is the way our culture has chosen, at one and the same time, to display and to disguise the female body. A woman's curves are given prominence as curves, but none of the organs that make those curves functional can be shown. In this way the image of woman is reduced to that of The Girl which Harvey Cox speaks of in *The Secular City:* the billboard queen who has nothing to offer men but stimulation.

The women I have consulted about this differ on how conscious they think women are of the effect their clothes have on men. Some think the problem belongs to the men, not to the women. "They don't have to look. If they get turned on, that's their problem. Nobody asked them to."

I think we would have to be deliberately naive in this age of psychological sophistication to ignore the fact that certain visual stimuli are objectively

226

and normally provocative to the sex drive of the
ordinary male. We might close our eyes to this, but
the merchants don't. And the fortunes they make
by putting their theories into practice prove they
know what they are doing. The clothes designers
we are speaking of, the advertising industry, and
the barons of pornography all know how to present the female body in a way that exploits the
sexual appetite of the male. All three present wom-
en to men in basically the same way, and all three
make money at it. Whether the women and girls
of our culture know or do not know what is going
on, they lose by it all the same. What is at stake
for them is their own identity and image as wom-
en.

I was once watching television with a friend
of mine: a married man with three children, a beautiful wife and a wild reputation. His nickname in
Dallas was "Bad Louis," and we were watching the
Dallas Cowboys. The halftime show came on.

This was before the Cowboys hired professional sex to match their own professional violence.
The halftime show was a marching band from a
college, with the usual baton-twirlers in leotards
prancing around the field.

As a celibate I was not too sure that my reactions were the same as the ordinary male's, so I
checked them out with Bad Louis.

"Louis, is there anything wrong with the way
those girls are dressed? The way they're marching?"

"Wrong?" he said. "No, nothing's wrong with
that. There's nothing wrong with that at all!"

"Louis," I said, "when your daughter goes to
college, if she became a drum majorette and dressed

and marched like that, what would you do?"

"I'd kill her."

Clearly, it makes a difference when you love someone. We are so used to accepting girls as sex objects we don't even notice it. But when there is question of making a sex object out of someone we love and look upon as a person, that is a whole new picture. Then we look at reality.

If our desire in human society is to respect and love one another as persons, then we can't help being concerned over the effect dress has on men, on women, and on their relationship to each other.

In the measure that a particular style of dress is consciously and deliberately provocative— whether the deliberate intent is on the part of the designer, of the wearer, or of both—this way of dressing must be recognized as a mild form of reverse rape by which a person arouses unsolicited sexual desire in another person who may not want to be aroused. Whenever this happens to men (who are more subject to this kind of arousal than women) it always causes some anger, whether recognized or not. This may explain some of the hostility and aggressive behavior that men are guilty of toward women. The men are hitting back.

Clean speech

One form this hitting back takes is obscenity. It is hard to think of any common slang word for sex which recognizes in any way that sex is an expression of love between two equal, self-bestowing persons. The slang words are usually degrading both to women and to the act of sex itself. Most frequently they are ugly in sound, crude in their imagery, demeaning in their implications.

Even though women in our society are increasingly using obscenity, too, I personally believe that obscenity is essentially a defense mechanism devised by males to reduce their sexual frustration. The male sex drive is experienced much of the time as just a compelling bodily appetite for physical gratification. When it is experienced this way it has nothing to do with personal expression; it is not associated at all with affection for another person. Men more easily than women can associate sex with pleasure for pleasure's sake and nothing else.

Of course no human being, whether male or female, can ever really dissociate sex in his or her mind from all that sex is meant to be, all the promise that it holds.

When people are put under the pressure of being simultaneously driven by physical sexual desires while prevented by circumstances from entering into any loving relationships, they try to cope with the situation by pretending to themselves that sex is nothing but a physical appetite.

When soldiers stand dozens deep in line waiting for a few minutes on the body of an overused prostitute to release their sexual tension, for instance, it doesn't help to think of sex as a personal act. Obscenity helps to reduce it to nothing but a physical function similar to, and almost on the same level as, the elimination of bodily wastes. When a combination of physical urge and circumstances drive a man to seek satisfaction within a whole context of ugliness, as in a whorehouse, one way for him to silence the repugnance in his heart is to talk as loudly and as constantly as possible of sex as if there were nothing there but ugliness and no response needed but callousness.

And this holds true, in proportionate degree, for the ugliness we experience as sin. We defuse the defacement of anything beautiful to ourselves by trying not to be conscious of how beautiful it really is.

The cumulative effect of obscenity is, I think, to help us keep up a brave front to ourselves in pretending that sex has no value anyway, so that we don't feel so bad about satisfying our physical desires in a purely physical way. But in the measure we succeed in this, we sacrifice our awareness of the meaning and value of sex. And this holds true for anyone—man, woman or child—for whom obscenity has become an acceptable pattern of speech.

Christians should react against this.

When St. Paul urges us, "Do not conform yourselves to this age but be transformed by the renewal of your mind," he is not encouraging us to despise our culture; he is teaching us how to love it. If we love it we will want to improve it. And if we want to improve our culture we must keep our own values clear.

Clean speech and modest dress may not sound like the most world-shaking of contributions, either to our own transformation or to the renewal of society. Some may wonder why we have given so much space to them here. It is because they are everyday values. What we wear and how we speak are habitual ways of acting that set the tone of our lives, not just occasionally, but all the time. They indicate and in part determine the level of our self-appreciation, of our respect for other persons, of our reverence and regard for the presence of God.

A girl who consciously dresses in a way that expresses the awareness she has of herself as the body of Christ is not readily going to speak, act, or let herself be used as a sex object. She is going to radiate a goodness that some might call wholesomeness, others beauty, and St. Paul calls the fragrance of the knowledge of Christ (2 Corinthians 2:14).

Likewise, anyone who keeps his speech clean in our society, especially in a male environment, is constantly going to be reminded, by that very fact, of his belief and his belonging to God. The very act of not conforming ourselves to this age is a reminder of the renewal of our minds.

If through the personal expression of Christians the people of our society ever stop saying to one another through dress that women are nothing but sex objects, and stop saying to one another through obscenity that sex is nothing but a physical release, our culture shall have come a long way.

18.

Language, Affection and Arousal
*The difference between romantic and
sexual touching (personal guidelines)*

Our last chapter gave us two principles which
roughly correspond to the physical and cultural
levels of our human existence:

1) On the physical level, because we recognize our capacity for sexual enjoyment as having
been given to us for a purpose, we never seek the
physical excitement of sexual pleasure as such outside of the relationship of marriage;

2) On the cultural level, because we recognize
the effect our self-expression has on other people—
as well as on ourselves—we want to express through
our speech, through our dress and in every other
way an attitude worthy of the full meaning and
value of human sexuality. We want to contribute
to our culture, not simply conform to it.

Now we want to deal with the problems that

arise in our personal expression of love. The principle which applies here is: Because we recognize sex as the language of spousal love, we never want to falsify our sexuality by giving any truly sexual expression to another until we are married.

This principle leaves us with the question, "Which ways of expressing affection are truly sexual and which are not?" Chapter 16 answered this question to some extent. In that chapter we saw that some actions are sexual by nature; namely, those which are biologically calculated to produce orgasm (e.g., sexual intercourse, heavy petting, masturbation), and those which, given the biological nature of human beings, could not reasonably be engaged in without the intention of producing or experiencing sexual arousal. We cited prolonged, heavy kissing as an example of this kind of action.

Where questions arise, however, is in the area of those actions which, while not necessarily sexual by nature, are ordinarily taken (and experienced) as sexual in a given culture. Just because an action is generally experienced as sexual in our society, it need not be experienced sexually by every individual person or in every conceivable set of circumstances. So how can we judge whether or not an action that is normally considered sexual in our society is truly a sexual action here and now for ourselves?

In Japan the whole family takes its bath together, along with any guests who may have dropped in for dinner. In New Guinea part of the rite of adopting a new man into the tribe is to have him suck on the breast of a young woman in simulation of nursing. In Africa grown men go on walks together holding hands. And in the German camps during World War II Russian prisoners slept naked together, jammed close in an effort to keep warm. All of these actions would have sexual overtones in our culture, but none are sexual in themselves; nor can they be presumed to be sexual as experienced in any of the examples I have given.

Among the Arabs, on the other hand, a veiled woman will not uncover her face to any man but her husband. To do so would be a sexual act for her as well as for him.

The fact that an action may not be sexual in itself, or in another culture, does not mean that we can make it nonsexual for ourselves just by waving the wand of our pure intention over it. Our cultural conditioning isn't something we can put on and off at will. The fact is, we are Americans, not Japanese. We live here, not in Africa.

Normally, if an action is considered sexual in our culture we must presume that we will experience it as such. Then we would have to have a pretty serious reason for engaging in it before we could say that our intention is not really characterized by a desire for sexual pleasure.

Is it ever legitimate for two people to express affection for each other through behavior that our society normally considers sexual?

I am not referring here to the kind of touching that we would all admit in our heads is nonsexual, even though our culture might make us uptight about it. Dr. Sidney Simon points out in the article I quoted in Chapter 16 that the college students he works with are not able even to massage a classmates's back in a gentle, caring way without joking and kidding first to dispel the sexual anxiety they feel about it. I am not speaking of this.

I am speaking about actions that no one would identify as just normal signs of caring in our culture: nakedness between the sexes, for example; touching parts of the body we associate with erotic simulation; actions that express extraordinary physical intimacy.

If we could trust ourselves and each other not to rationalize, we probably would not need any guidelines other than the ones we have already given. If we sincerely and deeply want to reserve all truly sexual expressions for marriage, and if we are honest with ourselves, we will probably remain authentic.

But people do rationalize; and we are people. And sex is a field in which we rationalize very well, at least as long as we are actually involved with someone physically or emotionally. Rationalization is usually in direct proportion to pressure.

During most of our lives the greatest pressure on us will probably be to conform to the business practices of our professional milieu—like those automobile designers in our country who rationalize on safety for the sake of greater profits and wind up with blood on their hands.

Prior to marriage we are pressured to conform in the area of sexual behavior. The way we handle the temptation to rationalize about sex while we are younger is a fair indication of the way we are most likely to handle the temptation to rationalize about ethics and honesty in business later on—and in everything else we do, unless we learn from our mistakes.

The guidelines I offer will not be useful to anyone who is still in the legalistic frame of mind that seeks justification through staying within bounds. People who are not directed from within by the light of an embraced ideal will be able to find loopholes in them. They are no substitute for sincerity; they are just a complement to conscience. They are not rules, but aids to our sense of direction. Like a compass, they won't keep us within bounds; they will only help us keep ourselves there if we want to.

Two rules of thumb

The first rule of thumb I would offer is this: *If what you are doing is something which, after you are married, you would not do with someone besides your spouse, then it is a sexual action and you should not do it until you are married.*

We may not be able to explain why, in every case, something is perceived by us as sexual. But we usually know what we would feel uncomfortable doing with a third party after we are married, or what we would not want our spouse to do with another person. If that is the way we feel about it, then we are recognizing that the action in question is more than a simple sign of affection. It is an expression of sexual love. It is not just culturally sexual. It is sexual for us.

If this sounds like a radical, unrealistic ideal, let's think about it for a moment. We have come to take for granted that a dating relationship will probably include a little sexual expression—very light sexual expression, perhaps, but a little bit of sex all the same. And as two people who are dating come to know each other better, we take for granted that they will become more physically involved. The more they like each other, the "further they will go" together sexually—up to a point, at least.

This whole attitude we have already challenged and rejected. Sex is not a scoring system, or a sliding scale of rewards for romantic attention given and received. Sex is a language that says something, something that cannot be said more or less and still be true at all. Sex is the language of spousal commitment.

We really know this in our hearts. That is why, if we were married, we would object not to the degree of sexual intimacy our spouse accepted with another, but to any truly sexual expression at all between another person and our husband or our wife.

After marriage we are very clear about what sex is. Before marriage we sometimes like to forget it.

Once we are married we want sex to be what it is, the language of spousal love, something unique between ourselves and our husband or wife. But before marriage we would like to find an excuse for tasting just a little bit of what we don't yet have a right to. And so we close our eyes to what sex means.

The second rule of thumb that I would offer sounds even more radical than the first, although in reality it comes down to the same thing. It is this: *Any action which you could not conceivably justify doing with your brother or sister, your mother or your father, is a sexual action and should not be engaged in outside of marriage.*

238

It's always fun to spring this principle on a group of high school students. The last time I did it was in a senior class where a girl in a front desk almost jumped out of her seat: "You mean I can't kiss my boyfriend any way I wouldn't kiss my brother?"

This is the reaction one would expect, and it is the normal one. When it comes I usually spend five or 10 minutes trying to get the class to notice the change that was introduced in my wording. The girl who repeated the principle didn't say the same thing I did. She changed a crucial word. I said *couldn't*; she heard *wouldn't*. That makes a great deal of difference.

The question is not what we *would* do with our brother or sister, but what we *could* do without thinking it improper.

Most American families are about as demonstrative of their affection toward each other as two fish who swim in different ponds. I know guys in high school who would not touch their sisters with a barge pole, and sex has nothing to do with it. They just do not touch.

But suppose you are a high school senior and your parents have gone to Europe. There is no one at home but your 15-year-old sister and yourself.

Suppose that your sister is kidnapped. She is missing three days. Then the police call you and say that they have found her: "Three men had her in an apartment. She's down here at the station now, and she's okay. Can you come and pick her up?"

You go down to the station. You don't know whether your sister has been raped or not, whether something really traumatic has happened to her, what kind of state she is in.

When you walk into the police station, would you just saunter up and shake hands?

Or would you take your sister in your arms and hold her, kiss her, make her feel loved, beautiful and safe?

I'll grant the case is extreme and somewhat dramatic. But it is meant to prove a point: There are a lot of actions you *would* not normally do with your brother or sister, but which you know you *could* do and not find anything sexual in them.

I can see two people on a date kissing in a way they would not kiss their brothers or sisters. This is not being sexual; it is being romantic. But if they kiss each other in a way they could not conceivably see themselves kissing a brother or a sister—under any circumstances—then they are kissing in a way that is sexual.

I would not want anyone to conclude from this book that two people who love each other cannot be romantic before marriage. Not only are people in love *going* to be romantic; they *should* be. But being romantic is not the same thing as being sexual.

Romance is not sex

An action becomes romantic because of the way people feel about each other. A sexual action is sexual whether the people feel anything for each other or not. With prostitutes, for example, men are sexual but not romantic. What is the difference?

A sexual action is arousing because of what it

240

is in itself, or because of what it says in the culture. People engaging in sexual actions either want to be aroused—and are seeking precisely that—or cannot reasonably expect not to be aroused while engaging in this particular action. Heavy petting is an example.

A sexual action might also be romantic, but if it is, the romantic element comes from the way the two people feel about each other, not from the action itself. For a young man and woman who love each other, heavy petting might be very romantic. But whether it is romantic or not, the action is still very sexual.

A romantic action, on the other hand, need not be sexual at all in itself. For a man and woman in love, holding hands can be very romantic. And sometimes it is sexually arousing! But here, if the action is arousing, it is not because of what the action is in itself, but because of the way they feel about each other.

If two people who are engaged, for example, should get sexually aroused while holding hands, just because of the depth of understanding, intimacy and love this touch might express between them, and because it reminds them of all they have promised to each other, and all that marriage holds in store for them, the arousal they experience does not make their action sexual. It speaks to them of sex because they love each other. In itself it only expresses affection.

The same is true for other actions. A high school boy kissing a girl for the first time in the moonlight is liable to feel sexually aroused, although probably not very intensely. The girl may feel arousal too. But the way they are kissing need not be sexual at all. They might be kissing one another in a way that many people kiss their mothers and fathers goodnight, or the way a very spontaneous, demonstrative girl might kiss her brother goodbye at the airport if he were going to be gone a long time and she loved him a lot. When boy and girl are kissing in the moonlight, what makes the kiss romantic—and sometimes sexually arousing— is not the kiss as such, but the moonlight and the way they are relating to each other.

This may sound like hair-splitting, but it isn't. One of the really sad things our culture sometimes does to us, I believe, is to condition us so thoroughly to associate romance with sex and vice versa that we can not distinguish between them. And what follows from this?

The first thing is that we do not know how to be romantic without being sexual. And the result of this, paradoxically, is that when we want to be sexual we do not know how to be romantic!

If we identify romance and sex, we will presume before marriage that the only way to touch each other romantically is by being sexual. Then, after marriage, we will make the same mistake by presuming that all sexual touching is romantic. It doesn't work that way. Marriage counselors are constantly having to explain to husbands that just getting sexual with a woman is not enough to make her feel romantic. But our society sets men up for this error.

In their first years of dating young people often do a lot of touching out of a kind of sexual curiosity. The boy wants to know what it feels like to touch a girl, and what her body feels like. The girl wants to know how it feels to be touched by a boy, and whether or not she has the power to attract him. Both are experimenting with their own sexual potential and with sex as such. At the same time they are lumping together in their own minds curiosity, sexual desire and romance.

Under the circumstances, touch is not an honest expression of affection. In part this is because neither the boy nor the girl has achieved enough integration of person and body, of feeling and expression, to let touch flow spontaneously from within. They are not yet mature enough to touch romantically; they don't really have for each other the depth of feeling and affection which romantic touching expresses. They are like actors on a stage reciting lines without any comprehension of the feeling that is supposed to go with them; they make the lines sound flat.

Another reason why touching fails at this stage is because it is too mixed up with other motives to be honest, authentic touching. It is too mixed up with sexual curiosity, experimentation and desire. It is ambiguous.

Both in the boy and in the girl there is probably enough ambiguity and mixture of motives to make the touching dishonest. But each is being dishonest in a different way. And because of this they wind up deceiving each other without intending or knowing it. A girl is more conscious of touching as an expression of affection, and a boy is more conscious of touching as an experience of sex.

As Dr. Mary Calderone explains: "Both the boy and the girl are seeking love and sex, but their needs are somewhat different. For the sake of clarifying the point, we can say the girl plays at sex, for which she is not ready, because fundamentally what she wants is love; and the boy plays at love, for which he is not ready, because what he wants is sex. We must understand that in reality both the boy and the girl seek love *and* sex, tenderness *and* passion, but that in the early years their drives are rarely synchronized" ("How Young Men Influence the Girls Who Love Them," *Redbook*, July, 1965).

As long as the touching that expresses romantic love and the touching we associate with sex are so identified that we cannot distinguish between them, this ambiguity between young men and women who date is practically insurmountable. If we distinguish between the two, however, and refuse to employ for romantic touching outside of marriage any action which is truly sexual in nature, then we will be free to learn how to touch—and touch romantically—without all this confusion.

Then a young woman will be able to trust that the young man she goes out with is really speaking to her through his gestures, and not just exploring to see how far he can get. She will know that his signs of affection are sincere, and not just an approach.

And men will learn how to use the language of touch in a variety of diverse and delicate ways to make the woman they love feel beautiful, appreciated and secure instead of just brushing over the keys in an impetuous prelude to sex.

According to Masters and Johnson, the bane of sexual relations in marriage is that couples do not know how to touch without being sexual.

"Many still think of it exclusively as a means to an end—touching for the purpose of having intercourse, a functional, wordless way to communicate a willingness, a wish or a demand to make love" ("Touching—And Being Touched," *Redbook*, October, 1972).

For other couples touch just becomes a means of stimulation, touch-as-technique. Through the sex manuals, Masters and Johnson report, "men and women are taught not how to touch another human being but how to manipulate another body." This impoverishes the whole marital relationship and sexual relations as a consequence.

"This is a dead-end approach to the sexual relationship," they maintain. "Preoccupation with manipulative technique turns persons into objects, and touching is turned into the science of stimulation. Instead of a sharing of private emotions, sex then comes perilously close to being an exchange of impersonal services."

Sexual touching need not be impersonal, of course. Touching for arousal—and this means touching that includes technique—can be extremely personal and romantic in marriage. But to make touch sexual and romantic at the same time the couple must be aware of touching as a language. And this is not easily learned if touching is always identified with sex. God made human beings, body and soul. He wants us to enjoy life, and enjoy it to the full. If we listen to the truth about ourselves as he teaches it, and follow the way he points out for us, it will lead us to the fullness of life. By reserving all truly sexual expression and experience for marriage, we are not going to impoverish our lives or our sexual enjoyment; we are preparing ourselves for a richer experience of both.

But more than that, we are living the truth of what we are and the truth of our relationship with God.

19.

The Goal of Perfect Freedom

Jesus as teacher, healer, savior of human wholeness (transcendent guidelines)

The verdict of one married woman who read the chapters up to this point was: "I agree with everything you've said, but anyone who can live this while dating is a saint."

That makes the ideals presented here sound a little impossible. But what if she had said, "Anyone who can live this would have to be Jesus Christ himself"? Then she would have been talking about what we are!

We are Jesus

We have already explained (see Chapters 7 and 14) that we are called not just to be followers of Jesus Christ. We are called not even just to imitate Christ. We are called to *be* Christ. The whole meaning and goal of our existence—the destiny we

have received from God—is to be the body of
Christ on earth. This is what St. Paul means when
he exhorts us, "Offer your bodies. . . . Be transformed. . . . Put on the Lord Jesus Christ and make
no provision for the desires of the flesh. . . . Both
in life and in death we are the Lord's" (Romans 12:1—14:8).

St. Paul doesn't urge us to base our life either
on reason or on rules; not even on the rules that
come from God himself. We should not go against
either reason or the rules, of course, but these only
keep us within bounds; they don't give the true
direction to our lives. When it comes to living the
fullness of life that is offered to us, and achieving
our real destiny, St. Paul tells us to let the knowledge of what we really are tell us what to do: "Use
the faith you have as your rule of life in the sight
of God" (Romans 14:22).

And what we are is the body of Christ, his
flesh on earth.

I once had to appear on a television talk show
with a visiting oriental who was a master of yoga.
Not knowing much about yoga and not wanting to
appear any dumber than I had to, I asked a young
man in the lobby of the studio who lived in a yoga
community just what it was all about.

"I know about the exercises," I told him,
"but explain to me your way of meditating."

He told me about taking a mantra and repeating it over and over.

"How does that change your life?" I asked
him.

"Well," he said, "Suppose my mantra is 'I am
an expression of the divine.' Suppose I am medi-

tating, saying it over and over to myself. Then suppose I go out to a record shop. I'm looking at the records and I see one I'd like to have. I think about ripping it off. But then the thought comes to me, 'An expression of the divine doesn't go around ripping off records.' So I don't take it. That's how the meditation changes my life."

I thought of the early Christians. The one thought that seems to have been always present to their minds—like a mantra embedded in their hearts—was the realization that they were the body of the risen Christ. Christ was risen and living in them through the gift of his Spirit. They were his body on earth. Their flesh was his. And that awareness guided all their moral choices.

We have already seen how St. Paul based his whole moral teaching on this truth. "You must know that your body is a temple of the Holy Spirit, who is within—the Spirit you have received from God. You are not your own. You have been purchased, and at a price. So glorify God in your body" (1 Corinthians 6:19-20).

This was the constant refrain of Paul's own heart: "The life I live now is not my own; Christ is living in me" (Galatians 2:20). "God himself can testify how much I long for each of you with the affection of Christ Jesus!" (Philippians 1:8). "In my own flesh I fill up what is lacking in the sufferings of Christ for the sake of his body the church" (Colossians 1:24).

And this was the center and core, the heart and soul of Paul's preaching as revealed in his Letter to the Colossians: He describes himself as sent to preach "that mystery hidden from ages and

251

generations past but now revealed to his holy ones. . . : the mystery of Christ in you, your hope of glory" (1:26-27). "In Christ the fullness of deity resides in bodily form. Yours is a share of this fullness, in him. . ." (2:9). "In baptism you were not only buried with him but also raised to life with him. . ." (2:12). "Since you have been raised up in company with Christ, set your heart on. . .things above rather than on things of earth" (3:1-2).

Being the body of Christ is not an ideal for us. Being Christ's body is just a fact; that is what we are. Living up to what we are is the ideal.

In the light of this it does not sound so unrealistic to embrace an ideal of sexual behavior that breaks entirely with many of the attitudes and values, many of the accepted practices of our culture, of our own peer group. Whatever is good in our culture, we accept. But we do not have to apologize to anyone for not conforming to those ways of thinking or acting in our culture that are contrary to the teachings of Christ.

Where our culture does not base itself on the mystery of our human call to be united with Christ as his body, we do not say our culture is *bad*. We just say it is unenlightened by the truth of Christ. Or, as St. Paul would say, the culture is, to that extent, in darkness. But we are not in darkness. We have been called into the light of Christ. And so we walk, not by the standards of the darkness, but by what we see through the light that has been given us. To do otherwise would be a denial of the light itself.

And we would fail to be for the world, and for our culture, what we are called to be: the light of the world, the salt that preserves and gives taste to our life upon earth. (See Matthew 5:13-16.)

"There was a time," St. Paul says to us, "when you were darkness, but now you are light in the Lord. Well, then, live as children of light. Light produces every kind of goodness and justice and truth. Be correct in your judgment of what pleases the Lord" (Ephesians 5:8-10). In the midst of our culture, St. Paul says, we should "shine like stars in the sky while holding fast to the word of life" (Philippians 2:15-16). We are called to be the "aroma of Christ" among men; God wishes to use us "to diffuse the fragrance of his knowledge everywhere" (2 Corinthians 2:14-15).

With this as our mission, we should not expect to "fit in"; we should expect to be "news" to our culture—the good news of Christ.

What all of this leaves us with is one final principle to guide us in our sexual behavior: *In everything we do, we should act as the body of Christ, conscious that the person we are with is also the body of Christ.* If there is anything we cannot feel comfortable doing while we are conscious of this, then as Christians we should not be doing it.

What if we fail?

If we try to live by this ideal, we will probably fail a lot. Then what do we do?

First of all, we must refuse to lower our ideals. If we fail and admit we have failed, our very failure can serve to confirm us in our desire to live by the ideals of Christ. Every confession of sin is a profession of faith. To say, "I was wrong in doing such-and-such," is to say at the same time, "I believe it

253

is right to do the opposite." But if we rationalize our failures, and bring our professed ideals down to the level of our conduct, we take away the very creative tension that helps us to grow.

Our society has become very guilt-conscious. Psychologists and counselors spend a lot of time helping people to deal with their guilt feelings. And many people do feel a false guilt they should not feel.

One thing many people find very difficult to understand is that real guilt does not make a person bad. In fact, experiencing guilt is usually a sign that a person is good. Feeling guilty is a way of looking down on something we have done. And we can't look down on anything unless something inside of us has already risen above it. Very often a person's realization of guilt is just a proof that his or her ideals are what they should be; that they are authentically high.

In such a case, to admit guilt is the first step toward getting rid of it. Rationalization never gets rid of guilt; it only suppresses it. What truly gets rid of guilt is forgiveness. The reason why Jesus Christ—and the Church in his name—can hold up to us an "impossible" ideal is because Christ in his Church also holds out forgiveness to those who fail.

Jesus was not just a teacher. Healing was something he combined with his teaching ministry from the very first moment that he began to proclaim the Kingdom of God. "Jesus toured all of Galilee. He taught in their synagogues, proclaimed the good news of the kingdom, and cured the people of every disease and illness" (Matthew 4:23).

And when he sent his disciples out to preach, he "gave them authority to expel unclean spirits and to cure sickness and disease of every kind" (Matthew 10:1).

Teaching and healing, then, go together in the Church. Christ in his Church can urge us to aim high because Christ in his Church can pick us up when we fall. The real healing Christ offers is not just healing of the body. Sickness of the body does not necessarily diminish life; it can often be the door to a fuller, richer life on the level of truly human existence.

What diminishes life is the inability to choose as we should. Every impairment to our freedom is an impairment of our ability to live. And this is the kind of affliction or sickness Christ really came to heal and still heals today in and through his Church. The miracles of physical healing were meant to be a sign of the greater miracle of healing which Christ offers to human freedom itself.

The despair of freedom

Whenever a counselor tries to relieve guilt feelings by telling a person that something objectively wrong is really not wrong in itself, that counselor fails to heal. What the counselor does is accept for the person a diminished level of freedom. The counselor is working out of the assumption that the ideal is beyond this person's reach, and is trying to make the person satisfied with a lower level of behavior. On the counselor's part this is essentially an act of despair.

It is one thing to teach a person that he or she should not expect to perform perfectly all at once. This is simple recognition of our need to grow. It is another thing, however, to deny an ideal as such. To do this is to despair of human freedom itself.

Counselors most often deal with sex in a person's life after some form of guilt-producing action has taken place. What the counselor is immediately concerned with is the feeling of guilt or shame that might be causing a disturbance in a young man or woman's life. And sometimes a counselor will deal with this by trying to convince the person that what he or she did is not really anything bad—that it was and is a normal, healthy, morally legitimate form of conduct in a young person trying to cope with his or her sexuality under the pressures of today's society. Instead of going to the source of the problem and teaching the person that some failure is normal in anyone trying to live the highest ideals, the counselor tries to deal with guilt by denying the failure itself.

But guilt and shame cannot be exorcised by a denial of right and wrong. The remedy for guilt is not to deny the evil. The remedy is encouragement and forgiveness, combined with acceptance of the person where he or she is.

This is something that anyone should be able to understand. But Christians in particular should understand it, because Christians have available to them in the Sacrament of Reconciliation the very special experience of forgiveness and healing that Jesus gave to those he touched. It is one thing to be assured by one's own interior spirit—or by a wise and holy person one consults—that God has forgiven one's sins. It is another thing to hear the voice of God himself speaking through a human voice that says, "Your sins are forgiven you; go in peace."

Because Christ offers forgiveness—and the experience of forgiveness that heals us and restores self-acceptance and joy—he can hold out to us an ideal that summons us to grow. This is the ideal of perfect freedom.

In the introduction to this book we quoted Eunice Kennedy Shriver's call for a new emphasis on moral values in the area of sex. Mrs. Shriver points out that we are talking about teenagers today as if they had no power of free choice. Later, in Chapter 4, we talked about the levels of freedom that correspond to the four levels of human life: physical, cultural, personal and transcendent. We said that what Jesus offers us is freedom through transcendence—a sharing in God's own vision of truth, and a new set of options based on the truth that God sees. These options lead to the fullness of life. "If you live according to my teaching," Jesus said, ". . . then you will know the truth, and the truth will set you free" (John 8:31-32).

Jesus does not reduce the goal of perfect freedom in any way. He does not have to lower the ideal, because perfect freedom is not just something Jesus preaches; it is something he gives. Jesus does not simply urge and exhort; he saves. And that is why his message is called the "gospel," which means not the "good advice" but the "good news."

The Good News is the event of Christ's own coming with power, to give us the strength and freedom we need to hear the word of God and keep it. That is why St. James exhorts us to "always speak and act as men destined for judgment under the law of freedom" (James 2:12).

The new law of Christ is measured to people who are presumed and empowered to be free. Freedom is God's gift to us; not to strive for it in its perfection is to refuse the very message of salvation.

We can be free

As Christians we do not have to accept any compromising, diminished ideal of sexual integrity, because as Christians we do not have to settle for any diminished notion of human wholeness. What we find held out to us in the gospel is "freedom's ideal law" (James 1:25). Jesus came that we "might have life and have it to the full" (John 10:10). We are saved from compromise by his promise.

Everyone who writes and speaks about sex as if a certain amount of premarital petting, or even a certain amount of premarital intercourse were just to be taken for granted—not just because statistically it is a fact, but because, realistically, nothing better can be expected of youth today—is implicitly denying the Good News of Christ. And if we ourselves ever accept this philosophy, then we are not only losing hope in the promise of Christ; we are giving up the struggle to be free.

There is nothing negative about an ideal of perfect integrity and freedom. But there is something very, very negative about accepting as a working principle that the best we can do about sex is give in a little bit and just try to keep from going all the way.

It is just as compromising to say that we would not have sex with just anyone, but that we think a little bit of sexual expression and enjoyment is all right with someone we really care about; or to use the rationalization that we are committed when in reality we know that we are not committed at all but free to break off the relationship any time we choose. What do all these compromises and rationalizations do to our understanding of sexuality itself? To what do they reduce its meaning and value?

And what do they say about us as persons? What unrecognized acceptance do they express of diminished personal freedom? Of diminished human wholeness and integrity?

If Jesus were just the Master of the Way, a teacher and model of perfect human wholeness, his contribution to our lives would be tremendous. But he is more than that. He is Savior—not just of our souls in the afterlife (although that is of crucial importance), but also of our humanity here on earth.

Because Jesus not only taught but healed—and still heals, through forgiveness, through the gift of strength and light, through incorporating us into the health and life of his own body on earth, through the favor of union with his own infinite power and love in grace—no one who believes in him has to settle for any diminishment of human life at all. And this includes the diminishment of human freedom, since for human persons to live is to be free.

20.

Being Whole to One Another
We are the credibility of Christ

Unity is the theme of this book: integrity and wholeness.

The goal of human living is to be our whole selves, complete and without division, in everything we do. We want to be "together" when we act.

This is the ideal of perfect freedom which we have been talking about. A country is not free, as a whole, so long as any segment of its population is oppressing any other segment. And a human being is not free so long as any part of his or her being is so dominant over the other parts that they are not able to be everything they ought to be, not free to function in the way that actualizes their full potential.

Our emotions can be so strong that they dominate our reason and keep us from thinking straight. Or reason can take over so much that we become "head people" who seem to have no emotions at all. The body can pressure the spirit to such a point that we just throw off all restraint and act like animals in much that we do. Or we can try so hard to be spiritual that, for all practical purposes, we make it seem that *flesh* is a bad word.

Christians are body-soul persons. For us the word of choice or of love that creates us as persons is not fully real until it has been made flesh in action. And the body, for the Christian, has no meaning or value apart from being the expression of the soul; that is, of a free, spiritual person whose existence in the flesh changes the body from a *what* to a *who*.

Yet all the personhood in the world is a hollow goal for Christians, nothing but a thin facade of meaning and value, if there is no ultimate fulfillment in life beyond death, life that will never end. An integral human being expresses in his or her behavior, then, not only the *what* and *who* of human existence, but also the *why* of the transcendent destiny to which we are called.

To be fully human means to live and act as the body of Christ. To have life and have it to the full means to integrate the human and the divine.

That is easy to say in the abstract. But when we translate this goal to concrete behavior in the real world, under the actual conditions of life as it goes on around us, the ideal of fully Christian living can appear very, very unrealistic. This is why we need the saints—and why we need to be saints for one another.

Saints: proof of what is possible

A saint is simply living proof that the grace of Christ works. The reason we need saints in every age is to demonstrate that the fullness of life as Christ offered it is achievable in every age. Saints are the truth of Christ made credible. They are the visible "now" of salvation.

The beauty and joy of the saints' behavior—and its manifest wholeness—proves that the ideals of Christ are valid, as Christ himself is valid, "yesterday, today, and forever" (Hebrews 13:8). No circumstances of time, of place, or of culture can make the teachings of Jesus, the Master of the Way, unrealistic. The grace of Christ is just as powerful now as it ever was, and his values can be lived in our day just as authentically as they have ever been lived, bearing the same fruit of wholeness, holiness and joy.

But the proof of this is people.

Nothing motivates us to an ideal so much as seeing that ideal realized and embodied in the life of another human being. When we see with our own eyes how effortlessly another person can play the guitar, for example, and hear with our own ears how good the music sounds, then we feel most motivated to practice the guitar ourselves. When we watch the Olympics on television and wonder at what others are able to do with their bodies, or go to a football game or tennis match and get turned on by speed and power and skill made flesh right in front of us, that is when we feel most inspired to get involved in sports.

For human beings seeing is believing. We are

inspired by what actually exists; and we believe that something is possible—or possible for us—when we see it realized in the flesh and blood of someone we can identify with.

God knows this. That is why he took flesh in Jesus Christ. He wanted us to see with our own eyes the beauty of God—his truth, attitudes and values—translated into human living.

This is why he gave us Mary, the perfect feminine embodiment of the beauty and love of God. In Mary we can see the beauty of God as a woman. And in her perfect response to God we can see the beauty of the fullness of grace to which we are called; we can see the goal of our own human response to Christ made flesh.

And this is why God gives us the saints, both ordinary and extraordinary, canonized and uncanonized. He shows us in the saints the life of grace being lived by human beings of every country and culture, of every race and age, of every variety of psychological temperament, intellectual ability and emotional predisposition.

The variety of the saints is the chief reason for their existence. There is no human being who cannot find a saint to identify with. No matter what our character might be, or the particular circumstances of our lives, or our previous history of sin, there is some saint who shows us what the grace of Christ can do for people like ourselves.

There have been geniuses like Catherine of Sienna and Thomas Aquinas; stupid saints like Joseph Cupertino, Bernadette of Lourdes and the Cure of Ars; rich saints like Thomas More and poor saints like Benedict Joseph Labre. Matt Talbot was an alcoholic who will probably be canonized some-day. One saint we know was called by God to be a soldier: Joan of Arc. And a whole crowd of ex-soldiers like John of God, Francis of Assisi, Ignatius of Loyola and Vincent de Paul became preachers, educators, missionaries and servants of the sick and poor.

John of God either left home or was kidnapped when he was eight and was on his own from then on. Joseph Cupertino's own mother didn't like him. Bernadette's family thought she was crazy. Ignatius of Loyola would start a street fight just to get room on the sidewalk. Margaret of Cortona was living with a man outside of marriage when he was killed in a robbery. And Theresa of Lisieux was a sweet, spoiled kid who never in her life did anything worse than pout.

Thomas Aquinas and Anthony of Padua were fat. So is Lucia, the only one still living of the children to whom Our Lady of Fatima appeared. Ignatius of Loyola was not only thin; he had stomach trouble. Jane Frances de Chantal was afflicted all her life with depression and doubts about the faith. Peter Canisius had a bad temper. And Peter the Apostle was scared to stand up for what he believed in, not only when he denied Christ on Good Friday, but also later when he played the hypocrite rather than stand up against a group of disapproving Christians (see Galatians 2:11 ff).

What all this tells us is that saints are nothing but sinners who kept trying. And their lives encourage us to keep trying for the highest and purest ideals of human behavior no matter how sinful we sometimes find ourselves to be.

Being saints for one another

There was a time when saints played the same role in Christian culture that athletes, movie stars and sex-symbols play in ours. The saints were the visible symbols of human success, the models held up for imitation. This is no longer true. The faces that used to appear in stained-glass windows and on religious medals have yielded to other faces that are silk-screened onto T-shirts, enlarged in photographs and mass-produced in media ads and commercials.

The stories American children are most exposed to are not the lives of the saints and martyrs but scripts written for television, laced with sex and violence to attract the widest range of viewers. The character traits of Kojak and Baretta, of Wonder Woman and Charlie's Angels are better known to most Americans than the virtues of Francis and Clare, of Ignatius and Theresa of Avila.

It isn't that our culture doesn't venerate its saints. It is just that another set of people are providing us with the images and models of salvation. Our towns are built around new temples; skyscrapers rather than cathedrals dominate our skyline. Our transcontinental pilgrimages are punctuated by hamburger stops, not by roadside shrines. And the images that dominate our consciousness are supplied for the most part by Madison Avenue, not by Michelangelo. No American is ever any farther away from eye contact with the symbols that express the commercial values of our culture than the medieval Christian was from the symbols that expressed the religious values of his. But in our culture business is more effective than religion in keeping its symbols before the public eye.

That is why we have to be symbols to each other. It is we, the visible body of Christ on earth, who must be living images and models of salvation to one another. We must do for each other in our time what the statues, pictures and stories of the saints did for people in the past. We must be the visible images of grace, the reminders of salvation to one another. We are called to show forth in our own lives something more attractive than sex and violence; something more appealing, even, than physical endowments, popularity and success. We are called to be the salt of the earth and the light of the world to one another.

St. Paul goes further than that. "God," he says, ". . . has shone in our hearts, that we in turn might make known the glory of God shining on the face of Christ" (2 Corinthians 4:6). That is our call: to let God live in us; to be the visible evidence—present, concrete and unmistakable—that his grace can and does triumph over all that would diminish human freedom. We must be the proof that it is possible to respond with perfect wholeness to the gospel in our own times.

The members of each sex have the potential to be models of wholeness to one another in particular, characteristic ways. These ways are the topic of the following chapters.

21.

How Women Help Men Become Whole
The oneness of person and body

Everyone knows that men and women are different, and most people rejoice in the fact. But given the spirit of our times, no one wants to say how men and women differ, or why they do, or whether it is really good that they should.

Some say that men and women do not naturally differ from one another in any way except in physical characteristics. All other differences, these people say—whether of psychology, personality or charm—are nothing but cultural conditioning. Others say that being a woman or a man as such means a lot more than just having a particular kind of body, and that this is much deeper than culture. But what concerns us is not whether the differences between men and women are biological, cultural, or both, but *how* men and women do actual-

269

ly differ in the present, real world—and how they can work with those differences in order to help themselves and one another be whole.

Whatever the causes, men and women generally do differ from one another in ways that can be identified. And in the measure that we can identify these ways, each sex will be helped to understand a little better what it has to work with, and what it can work toward.

I think that men and women each have special advantages and special disadvantages in their efforts to be whole. Women grow up in our society blessed with a particular oneness of soul and body that men admire and want to preserve in women, but find difficult to understand or to achieve for themselves. Men, on the other hand, grow up being one with themselves in another way which women recognize as both different and complementary to their own experience.

As men and women interact deeply with one another, each learns from the other how to become what he or she is not. And in this way each sex helps the other to be whole. At least this *can* happen if men and women interact on a basis of respected complementarity rather than of conflict.

Men and women begin life experiencing the wholeness of their persons in different ways. Girls, for example, are brought up to be one with their bodies in a way that boys are not. This leads a girl to center her value within herself, in what she is, rather than in what she can do.

From their earliest years girls are dressed up and everyone tells them how pretty they are. This can have the bad effect of making a girl think her value is just in her appearance, and of making her depend for her self-image on the way others respond to her. But it also has the good effect of helping women to realize—better than men do, at least—that the worth of human beings is not really measured by how much they accomplish, but simply by what they are. Being is more important than doing. And it helps to give women, as they are growing up, a sense of oneness with their bodies. Women identify personally with their bodies; what touches their bodies touches their selves. The self and the body are one in the psychology of a woman.

Boys grow up quite differently.

A boy acquires the impression quite early that his body is simply an instrument for him to use. His body is his weapon, his tool. His task is to strengthen it, harden it, train it, and then go out and do something with it. His value is in what he can do, not in what he is in himself.

Men, as a result, do not grow up feeling one with their bodies. The self, for a man, is the thinking, ruling voice in the control tower, the detached spirit who decides and chooses what the body will do. In an oversimplified generalization we can say that while a woman *is* her body, a man just *uses* his.

Girls are encouraged to express themselves with their whole bodies. They can cry and dance and hug and kiss with a spontaneity not allowed to boys. Girls can squeal with delight, jump up and down, agitate their hands, and use every tone of their voices from normal speech to high C in conveying their emotions. A woman's body is a medium of expression.

271

Boys use their bodies not so much to express themselves as to express the determination they have not to express themselves. Except, perhaps, for anger, which is a very functional emotion, a man doesn't let his person appear in his flesh. His body is a shield that hides his feelings.

In our society, and probably in most human societies, cleanliness is emphasized for girls more than for boys; not only cleanliness of the body, but cleanliness of dress and of speech as well. For a woman, everything about her body is expressive of herself: the way she looks, fixes her hair, the clothes she wears, the language she uses. It is important to her, therefore, that the outside match the inside.

For a man, since the body is just an instrument anyway, how it looks is not all that important as long as it is kept fit and functional. A man feels very presentable covered with sweat and blood—coming off the field, for example, after a football game. He likes to be seen that way, especially by his girlfriend. A woman in the same condition would rather shower before she talks to anybody.

The same thing is true of speech and even of sexual activity. Since a man does not identify his body with his person as much as a woman does, he doesn't consider the words and actions of his body to be the direct expression of his self. What his body does is one thing; who he is in himself is another. If he uses bad language, the words he speaks have little to do with his person. They are like mudballs he picks up and throws. Sex, too, can be a very impersonal act for a man.

But this is not true of a woman. Her words are the direct expression of her person. They reflect her heart and reflect back on the image she has of herself. A woman cannot dissociate—as easily as a man does—the words and actions of her body from the ideals and reality of her soul.

For a woman, in other words, her body is the natural medium for the expression of her heart. For a man it is a tank to drive around in.

All of this explains in part why women attach so much value to their bodies, and are much more private about them than men are. Girls are taught to treat their bodies as something precious, even sacred. Modesty, or a sense of privacy with regard to one's own body, is something girls are allowed and encouraged to have, even in the presence of other girls. The opposite is true for boys.

It was a shock to me in high school when I learned that girls, in their locker rooms, had individual stalls for showers. In our school, after sports practice, the boys took showers in one big room; there was no privacy at all and no one even thought about it. All the boys I knew had been swimming naked together from their earliest years. Bathing suits, in fact, were officially discouraged in the Y.M.C.A. pool, in our town's athletic club, and in one summer camp I went to. I never knew until high school, when a girl I was dating told me, that girls were not equally unreserved in the presence of other girls.

I really do not know whether the way women feel about their bodies is natural to them or whether they are trained to it; just as I do not know whether the alienation men feel from their bodies is natural or induced by culture. Whatever the answer, it does seem that most human cultures encourage the distinction. And there may be a reason for it.

The divided male

In primitive societies—and ours is not substantially different in this—men have to go to war and stick swords and spears into other people's bodies. In a situation like that, the more you identify the body with the person, the more traumatic your occupation is going to be.

The work men do, now as in times past, frequently exposes them to a much greater risk of getting banged up, scarred or maimed than the work women do. If a man attaches too much value to the prettiness of his body, he is set up for a lot of psychological pain if he is injured.

Because men are sent out in armies and work gangs for extended periods of time, men frequently find themselves living under conditions that make modesty, privacy and sometimes even cleanliness impossible. Men in barracks and work camps, living outdoors or on the road, would find life very difficult if they were accustomed to bodily privacy and attached importance to it.

It may well be that the instinctive, perhaps unconscious response of human cultures to this situation has been deliberately to train men, from boyhood up, not to identify too closely with their bodies and not to be conscious of them as sacred.

It may also be that one reason for the high degree of obscenity that is usually found where large numbers of men live and work together is

274

that obscenity is an unconscious defense. Men prevented—or hindered, at least—by circumstances from acting in a way that recognizes the sacredness of human flesh and its functions tend to relieve their frustration by making a joke of everything that is physical. Even sex is spoken of in terms of purely physical satisfaction or in gaming terms as if there were no other value in it, no deeply human or personal dimension involved. This is an understandable coping reaction, even if it is destructive, in men who have to deal with their sexual desires under circumstances that allow them no normal, personal relationship with women.

It may be, then, that for all of these practical reasons human cultures have deliberately trained men not to be one with their bodies, and not to attach much value to them except as weapons or tools. But the practical gain in fostering such an attitude in men, if it really is a gain at all, is offset by a corresponding loss in personal wholeness. And for this reason, the more men are brought up to be in any way divided from or alien to their bodies, the more they wonder at, admire and delight in the oneness women have.

It would almost seem that the less a society is able to allow its men to preserve a sense of sacredness about their bodies, the more it tries to encourage this sense of sacredness in women.

Men who themselves are forced to work all day in physically dirty surroundings, among other physically dirty men, have a special appreciation for the cleanliness of body and dress they find in a woman. Men obliged to take obscenity for granted all around them the whole day long find relief in the presence of a woman who not only does not take it for granted but is visibly offended by it.

There is a wholeness, a sense of the sacred, a unity of body and person in women that men are drawn to as to something beautiful and lacking in themselves. Whether the culture develops this in women, or whether it is innate to them and society has simply allowed them to retain it, it does exist. Men recognize this wholeness in women, value it, delight in it and sometimes publicly honor it. Wherever it is not present they notice and regret its loss.

The age-old double standard comes in for a lot of criticism these days. The double standard is presented as an attitude which says that certain forms of sexual behavior, obscenity and so on are okay for men, but not okay for women. *Newsweek* magazine (April 6, 1964) cites as an example of this attitude the Columbia University senior who, when asked whether or not he was in favor of intercourse before marriage, replied with the question, "For me—or my kid sister?"

I believe that, by and large, when people say that some form of sexual behavior is okay for men but not for women they are not really saying it is *morally* okay for men. They are saying it is *less damaging* to men. Men don't have as much to lose by it—either for the obvious reason that men don't get pregnant, or for the less obvious reason we present here. Women have a oneness of body and person to lose which men cannot lose because they don't have it to begin with.

The Columbia student quoted in *Newsweek* would probably have said, if questioned further, that he thought his little sister was "more pure" in her thoughts, desires and conduct than he was. He probably could have added that he thought she was more idealistic about the meaning and value of sex than he was, and that he didn't want to see her disillusioned. Or that she attached a lot of value to her body's expression while he felt rather cynical about the value of his own.

Helping men to appreciate themselves

The double standard is not so much a moral principle as a recognition of the fact that women are blessed with a certain goodness and beauty, a oneness of body and person which it would be a shame for them to lose. It would be nice if men had this oneness, too, but they do not as a general rule, and their role in society does little to help them acquire it.

The most likely way men will grow into that oneness is through seeing it concretely realized in women they love and admire. Women can give to men a richer appreciation of what it is to exist as body and soul, and help men bring spirit and flesh into oneness. Men feel the need for this so much, whether consciously or not, that they try in a multitude of ways, both valid and misguided, to keep women from becoming exactly like themselves.

A woman who retains her wholeness and her sense of oneness with her body can teach a man she loves to appreciate himself, to value who he is rather than just what he can do. She can help him discover his body as a medium of self-expression rather than just a machine for working, fighting and pleasure. She can introduce him to a whole dimension of physical expression and tenderness that he may only barely appreciate. She can draw out of him the expression of emotions he customarily suppresses or keeps stoically to himself. She can give him a confidence in himself and in his personal value that no accomplishment and no other person or thing has ever been able to give him.

But she can only do this by remaining a woman, by preserving and developing the oneness of her body and person that both awakens a man's wonder and commands his respect. She must embody within herself the dimension of wholeness that is particularly hers. And this involves a special respect for her body and everything associated with it.

22.

How Men Help Women
to Completeness
The voice in the control tower

The strength of men, as we might expect, is the counterpart of their weakness. Because men are not one with their bodies, they do not trust them. For the same reason they do not trust their emotions. They tend not to identify their personal selves with any spontaneous, physically-felt reaction. This forces them to fall back constantly on the objectivity of reason and to identify their persons with the exercise of deliberate choice. This is men's strength as well as their weakness.

The alienation of men from their bodies may be culturally fostered, but there is biological cause for it also. When a boy reaches adolescence he begins to feel physical sexual desire which has nothing to do with affection for any person. A boy desires physical intimacy and specifically sexual gratification with any and every girl he sees who is normally attractive. He does not have to know a girl in order to want to caress her, kiss her, or have intercourse with her. The mere fact that a girl walks across the street in front of him is enough to arouse his physical desire, especially if her sexual characteristics are emphatic.

This experience confirms the boy in what he already took for granted: that his body and physical appetites have very little to do with his person. If he could articulate the subconscious argument in his mind, it would probably go like this: "What has my body got to do with my person if it goes out in sexual desire for a girl I don't even know?"

More specifically, he probably begins to take for granted at the same time that sex itself has nothing to do with his person, since his sexual desires don't seem to depend on any personal relationship. His appetite for sex is like his appetite for food. It reacts to stimuli on its own, independently of his personal attitudes, decisions or choices.

Girls experience physical desires too, of course. But to a much greater degree their sexual desire is connected in their minds with personal relationship, with being loved. While a boy wants to kiss, to touch, to explore, to have intercourse with the female body as such, regardless of whose it is, girls do not usually want to be kissed or touched unless they find some personal meaning in it.

As a consequence, men do not have the spontaneous, almost innate appreciation of the meaning and value of sexual expression that women do.

There is danger that men will look upon sex as a purely physical thing, hardly making a connection between their bodily actions and any personal expression of themselves.

On the other hand, and for this very reason, men are more likely than women to judge correctly the whole, objective situation in which their sexual activity takes place.

Sex is a natural language for women. Because women understand their value as within themselves, their understanding of love is to make a gift of themselves. And because they are so at one with their bodies, the surrender of the body in sex speaks to them by its very nature of love and the gift of their person.

For this reason, women can too easily take for granted that something which feels so much like love and—in their language—speaks so much of love must be love in fact. This frequently keeps women from asking the hard, objective questions, either about the reality of their own commitment or about that of their partners. Where there is a satisfying experience of sex and the feeling of giving themselves completely to another, love and commitment seem so obvious that they feel no need to ask.

For men, on the other hand, sex is not a natural language (until they learn it), but commitment is. And commitment is expressed in service.

Men have been taught from childhood to locate their value, not in what they are in themselves, but in what they can do. It follows that their understanding of love is to do something for the person they love: to work for that person, fight for her, take care of her, supply all her needs.

When Dagwood rushes out the door on his way to work without kissing Blondie good-bye, he is acting like a man. When, however, he remembers halfway to the bus stop that he hasn't kissed her good-bye and rushes back to do it, he is acting like a married man who understands women.

For Dagwood the kiss means very little; the way he shows love is by working for his wife downtown. For Blondie the kiss is important; she knows that without it Dagwood may be working downtown, but he won't be working consciously for her, at least, not for very long. Both Blondie and Dagwood are right, and both have to learn from each other. They start from opposite ends of the same reality and help each other to move toward the center and wholeness.

Men center on commitment

A woman centers on love as a felt experience and takes commitment for granted. A man centers on commitment and takes the feelings of love for granted. For a woman, sex means love and self-gift; therefore sex means commitment. For a man, love and self-gift are identified with commitment as such, and therefore sex doesn't mean anything at all until the reality of commitment is established. For a woman the dignity of sex can be experienced in the actual, physical giving of herself. For a man the dignity of sex comes from the fact he has already given himself through some other, objective commitment.

Men do not spontaneously think of their own sexual act as an expression of self-gift. At its least generous, it is an act of physical indulgence. At its most generous, it is a way of giving pleasure to their partners. Even in sex men tend to be functional achievers, at least until they learn to use sex as a language that can become an expression of themselves.

But the language men naturally understand is commitment. And commitments must be concrete to be real. Love and self-gift are nothing but words to men until they are spelled out in commitment to specific, concrete actions. It is precisely the commitment to serve another that spells the difference between the real love of a man and the romantic preliminaries of a boy; and every male is aware of this.

Until such commitment is a fact, men know that any claim they make to love another is still an unproved assertion. Love is proved by deeds. Until a man has done something for the woman he loves, or committed himself to doing something for her, anything he says to her about love is in the airy realm of poetry. Action brings assertion down to earth. It is in the actions they commit themselves to, therefore, that men find the dignity of love.

What ultimately makes sex an experience of self-gift for a man is the realization that the only reason he can take his wife's body to himself is because he has already, through marriage, taken her unto himself to feed and clothe, to work for and protect, to share his inmost thoughts and feelings. Then every act of taking his wife's body to himself is a reaffirmation and reminder of his own dedicated gift of self to her.

Sex is meaningful to a man because he is committed. But it would never occur to a man to think he is committed just because sex is meaningful.

A man doesn't assume that because he wants to experience a woman sexually he loves her. He is too aware that, whether he loved her or not, he would want to experience her sexually. And so he tends to see sex as one thing and love as another, and to ask questions about each independently. It doesn't enter his head to conclude that because he wants to embrace, fondle, kiss or have intercourse with a woman, therefore he must love her. This is one reason why a man cannot argue convincingly—with other men, at least—that because he loves a woman it is therefore appropriate to have sex with her.

A boy might use this last argument with a girl, sensing that for her it will be persuasive. And he might even use it, rationalizing, with himself. But the argument does not have roots in his psychology; it pulls out easily and cleanly when a little effort is applied.

Compare these two reports:

"Sally was an especially gifted student, interested in her work, and gave promise of a successful creative career. In high school she had had her eye on getting into a good college. She had not been active in the social life of school, which seemed to her superficial. In her freshman year at college, she threw herself into a whirl of active dating, received many invitations, and was very popular. When she had satisfied herself that she was desirable and could carry off social occasions well, some of the excitement of dating began to pall and she sought more meaningful relationships. She now dated only boys with whom she felt she could establish a deeper emotional and intellectual relationship. One of the boys she came to know better wanted to have sexual relations. She described her reaction: 'For me it is a special thing. I am sort of monogamous. I don't like to diffuse to a lot of people. I like to have close friends even though I know a lot of people. As far as I am concerned, intercourse is one thing where you are giving a lot of yourself to one person. I never wanted to do it unless I was absolutely sure about that person and I never was; particularly when I started realizing that these people did not care much about my welfare or about me as a person. It impressed me as if they almost had to prove to themselves and also to other people that they could do it. It was a competitive thing.'

"Sally had not expected to engage in sexual relations in college. In her junior year, however, she met a boy who, she said, was 'interested in my interests, and I was interested in his interests.' Eventually, they had intercourse. Here is her description of her feelings: 'It got to the point where it really got frustrating not doing it. We had been going out together seven or eight months and it seemed—if you feel strongly about a person and if you really love him—I don't see anything really wrong about it, because it is a complete relationship, as complete as for some people who get married. This is one action where you give everything you have to the other person. There is always a circumstance of holding back and it would have been wrong; it would have been almost wrong to keep holding back something that I really wanted to give him.' " (Group for Advancement of Psychiatry, *Sex and the College Student*, Report Number 60, Chapter 2, "Sexual Issues on the Campus.")

The reason why Sally had intercourse is that it seemed the natural thing to do, given the way she felt about the boy she was dating. For her, love and sex went together. To give herself in love without giving herself sexually seemed to her like a "holding back," and "almost wrong," since it was "something I really wanted to give him."

She was not asking the question independently about the nature of the love they had for one another, whether it had in fact reached the stage of a decision to marry, whether the commitment was a real one, or what kind of commitment it was. She was more aware of the connection between love and sex than she was of the independent reality of each. Her decision to have intercourse was an affirmation of the oneness of her body and her person, but it passed over the equally important question of whether or not the personal relationship being expressed in physical language was in fact as real as the language said it was.

The report doesn't tell us whether or not Sally and the boy she had intercourse with were eventually married to each other. If they were not, then we have to raise the question of what this first experience did to Sally's own natural association of love and sex. She was able to give herself naturally and spontaneously to the boy she loved because of the oneness of her body and her person. To love and to express love were all one with her, which was her special endowment as a woman. But if, as a matter of fact, she learned through hard experience that no real, actual commitment had ever in fact been present—either on her side or on the side of the young man—when she gave herself so spontaneously, would she ever be able to trust again—in the same natural, easy way, at least—in the oneness of her body and person in sex?

Let us look at a second report, this time from the viewpoint of a male college student:

"I met a girl and started making love to her. Eventually she fell in love with me. (At least she thought she loved me and that, I think, amounts to the same thing. In other words, she could be badly hurt.) One day we were alone in my father's home and we decided to make love. This we accomplished in a bedroom on the second floor. After we finished, she wanted to be kissed and to hear that I loved her—anything at all that would justify the act. What she did not know was that I felt nothing but a physical attraction for her and wanted no part of her after we were finished. . . . For the first time I realized the damage I had done." (Phyllis and Eberhard Kronhausen, *Sex Histories of American College Men*, Ballantine Books, 1960.)

Our first reaction might be to characterize the young man in this report as unfeeling, insensitive and exploitative. He comes through as just using the girl, which is in fact what he was doing.

But we should pay a lot of attention to the last sentence of the report: "For the first time I realized the damage I had done."

This is a frank, nondefensive confession. What it reveals is that when the boy actually had intercourse with the girl he really did not understand

289

what this was saying to her. He probably felt that if he had deceived the girl at all it was in telling her beforehand that he loved her. More than likely he did tell her this, in some form or another, in order to persuade her to give in. But he obviously did not comprehend at all how much the act of intercourse itself expressed love to this young woman. It would never have occurred to him that his sexual gestures themselves were a lie. And he certainly did not dream that the girl was interpreting all the passion of his sexual act as a passion of affection for her.

If he did know in fact that he was deceiving her, he had no idea how deeply she was being deceived. He could have told her many times he loved her without the word meaning anything more to him than a general expression of appreciation and affection. Had she asked him specifically whether he loved her enough to marry her, and whether in fact he was committing himself to do so, he would have honestly told her no.

To his way of thinking, nothing he had said to the girl up to that point gave her any reason to assume that their relationship was really serious. What he did not understand was that, to her way of thinking, intercourse would say just this.

The damage men can do

This young man discovered that, for a woman, the sexual act itself is the expression of a love as deep and as passionate as the emotions it arouses. A woman simply does not understand how completely a man is able to distinguish between the passion of his physical and emotional response and the real involvement of his person. When a woman having intercourse *feels* the gift of self, she is *making* the gift of self—or at least she tends to believe she is. This is so natural to her that it is just inconceivable to her that a man could have intercourse and not be expressing his gift of self— or not be drawn through it, at least, to make the gift of himself.

Dr. Mary Steichen Calderone attempted, in a talk to Notre Dame University students, to explain to men how much damage their sexual behavior can do if they do not understand how women think. Young men, said Dr. Calderone, are generally unaware of the impact they have on the development, the personal growth, the emotional unfolding and flowering of the young women they date. As a result their behavior is frequently irresponsible and destructive without their even being conscious of it.

What frees a girl to express the sexual side of her nature, Dr. Calderone explained, is "her belief that the boy loves her and that she loves him." A man can exploit this if he wants, playing at love consciously and lightly—not necessarily in a way that is totally false, but not in a way that is totally sincere either—with the goal of arriving at sex.

A girl cannot do this the way a male can, Dr. Calderone insists. She has greater need for "a feeling of legitimacy" about her behavior before she can give herself sexually to a boy. For this reason, if a girl plays at love it is in a more profound and vulnerable way. Before she can give herself sexually she has a need to believe in love. If the love is not real, it is herself, not the boy, whom she must deceive. But the danger in this is enormous.

A boy can assist a girl in this deception, even by just encouraging in her presumptions about his feelings toward her which she may be all too willing to make. When he does so, he can do her more harm than he can imagine.

As Dr. Calderone expressed it: "I believe that every young man needs to know and to accept the fact that because he plays a crucial role in furthering a young woman's emotional maturity, he must accept also the responsibility that goes with it. He must understand that the sexual act for a woman tends to be the ultimate expression of what she feels about life and her belief in it, expressed through her love for and belief in the man with whom she chooses to live the rest of her life. If she engages in sexual experience before she is mature enough, sex may become an end in itself—or the ability to enjoy sexual experience may be crippled forever—and her capacity for a deeper relationship arrested forever." (From a talk given at Notre Dame University, printed in *Redbook*, July, 1965.)

A man's strength lies in his ability to distinguish between feeling and commitment, between his emotional experience and the reality of his personal choice. He is very much in touch with his intellect and will; the oneness he experiences as a human being is a oneness of person, understanding and choice. The very alienation a man suffers from his body and his emotions helps him to retain an objectivity regarding them.

His task as he matures is to integrate his body and emotions into the oneness of his personality so that he may be completely whole. It is essential for him, however, while he does this, not to lose his objectivity but to retain the oneness with his thinking, choosing self that is his masculine endowment. When a man begins to separate sex from objective commitment, he is losing the strength of his manhood.

This is a point that women should reflect on. Men find no dignity in sex unless it is the expression of commitment. Whenever a woman allows a man to have sexual relations with her—even if the action does not go as far as intercourse—she is stripping his sexuality of its dignity. She is giving him something for nothing. She is letting him take her body without taking responsibility for it. She is encouraging him to remain a child.

Small wonder that so many men in their married lives fail to take up the responsibilty of being husbands and fathers. If from the very beginning of their dating relationships they have become accustomed to taking from women without taking on responsibilities, much of what sex could say to them in marriage may be lost. The awesome gift of a woman's body to them in intercourse may not have the power it should to draw forth from them a corresponding gift of responsibility and care.

Responsibility in marriage is built on other things than sex, of course. But sex is too integrally a part of marriage for its particular power to be sacrificed without significant loss. If a man's physical enjoyment of his wife in marriage is not associated in his mind with the vows he pronounced before God and the whole world on his wedding day, promises which made him a husband and head of a family, then sex will not be for him the reminder, the reaffirmation and the strengthening that it should be of his commitment to assume responsibility.

Sexual relations may just be for him a pleasure he feels he has a right to because he happens to be married. If this is the case, he will remain basically immature in his sexuality, a boy instead of a man, and this same immaturity may characterize his whole relationship in marriage.

Why girls must say no

Girls find it hard to say no to the boys they are dating. Both in my own counseling experience and in the reports I have read, this seems to be the one most common cause why girls have sex before marriage, whether we are speaking here of intercourse or of some level of sexual stimulation that stops short of going all the way.

It is true boys put pressure on girls, overriding a girl's convictions and ideals, wearing her down with arguments and rationalizations the girl is unable to answer, accusing her of being cold, or hung up, or lacking in love and affection if she doesn't give in and conform to what the boy wants to do. And for this the boy is to blame; he is not respecting his date as a person, not leaving her freedom intact.

But how much blame should girls be willing to accept for allowing this? How many girls, when they are dating, suppress their own beliefs and ideals about sex and other things in order to please the boy they are with? How many give in to their date's desires without insisting that the boy face up to and respect their own attitudes and values, their own feelings about what they are doing, equally with his own?

Seventeen magazine reports this dialogue between a counselor and a 16-year-old girl in New York City:

Girl: My boy friend wants me to take the Pill so we can have sex.

Martinez: Do you want to?

Girl: Not really. But I don't want to hurt his feelings.

Martinez: Does he like you a lot?

Girl: I think so.

Martinez: Then how come he's hurting your feelings? (Alice Lake, "A Girl's Right to Say No," June, 1974.)

If boys are to blame for not respecting enough the feelings and convictions of the girls they date, girls are equally to blame for letting boys do this, thus giving boys the impression that a woman does not have any attitudes or values which a man should take seriously or respect.

How can a boy be expected to know that the girl he is dating has deep convictions if she is not willing to insist that he respect them? And if a girl submerges her own feelings about things in order to please the boy she is with, how is she preparing the boy to face up to and respect his wife's feelings—or her attitudes and values—concerning all the issues of their married life later on? How can a boy who has become accustomed in dating to getting whatever he wants without any serious confrontation of his girlfriend's convictions or desires be expected to relate to his wife any differently?

The title of the article we cited above from

Seventeen is significant in itself: "A Girl's Right to Say No." No one would think of writing an article about a boy's right to say no, because it would never occur to a boy that he had to give up that right. But girls feel a tremendous pressure to give in to the boys they are dating, even if it means giving up the right to follow their own convictions and ideals.

Our sympathy is naturally drawn to the girls, because we understand very well the pressures they are under. But I think we should direct some of our concern toward the boys who are thus encouraged while dating to think that their own convictions and desires are the only ones that count, only to find after marriage that their wives now want to discuss all principles and decisions with them as equal partners. The girl who gives in to a boy before marriage just for the sake of pleasing him is helping to set the pattern for that same boy's future relationship with his wife. She does as much harm to him by giving in to his desires as he does to her by putting on the pressures.

One thing girls can be certain of: A boy knows what he is doing, and he knows that it is wrong. The age-old saying is still true: Boys respect girls who are able to say no.

Seldom, if ever, have I heard a boy say in confession that he is having sexual relations with a girl, but that he just can't believe it is wrong because he loves her. What I hear more often is the boy who says he knows it is wrong but that when he is with a girl who is willing, then whether he loves her or not, he is just unable to resist.

Initially, of course, the boy yields to his own

sexual desire in testing to see if the girl is willing, or how far she is willing to go. Under the pressure of a here-and-now temptation the boy will rationalize what he is doing in every possible way. But later he has no doubt that it was wrong.

Nevertheless, once it is established that a particular girl is willing to allow him a particular level of physical, sexual intimacy he finds it all but impossible to hold back from going that far if he takes her out at all. Every sexual yielding on a girl's part opens a gate which it is almost impossible afterwards to close. The tragedy is that one young man after another has told me he had to decide to stop dating a girl he really liked as a person, just because he knew that with her he would be unable to keep himself in check.

When men and women sin sexually, they handle the conscience problem in different ways. Both in reality are dividing themselves, separating their physical behavior from the moral judgment of their intellects. Both are, in fact, denying their sexuality by falsifying the true meaning and value of their sexual expression. But they have different ways of resolving their inner conflict.

The boy does it by admitting his action is wrong, but denying that it is important. Since the body does not involve his person, he figures that what he does with his body cannot be all that wrong. When he sins he sacrifices his body to his passions but keeps his reason clear.

The girl does just the opposite. The expression of love through her body is so important to her that she cannot believe it is wrong. Since her body does involve her person so deeply, she feels that whatever she does with her body while feeling it to be authentic cannot be anything but right. When she sins she identifies her person with her feelings and tunes out her reason as an alien voice.

If they both learn the hard way, the boy will realize his guilt the way the college student we quoted earlier realized his: by seeing how much damage he has done to a girl who trusted him. This wounds the boy in his self-image precisely where it is most important to him. He loses respect for himself as a strong, responsible personality guided by intellect and will. Having become accustomed to identifying his person with the "voice in the control tower," he now holds himself responsible for a wreck.

The girl, on the other hand, has grown up delighting in the oneness of her body and person. Now she sees herself as divided, her physical expression separated from the ideals and values of her heart. If the boy sees himself as responsible for a wreck, she sees herself as the wreckage.

This naturally makes the admission of sin more shattering to a girl, and it does, in fact, take girls longer to admit it. But when any of us, men or women, do admit our guilt, the strength of another man comes into play: Jesus Christ who is able to say, "Your sins are forgiven; be made whole."

For men and women alike, all sin is an acceptance of division, just as all sin is a loss of personal freedom. But Jesus said:

You will know the truth
and the truth will set you free. (John 8:32)

He also said:

>   I came
>   that they might have life
>   and have it to the full. (John 10:10)

Neither men nor women are perfectly whole to begin with; oneness is something we grow into. And we are called to this: not only to become one with ourselves, but to cooperate with the Spirit of God in bringing all things into unity. For this, St. Paul tells us, is the design of God: "to be carried out in the fullness of time: namely, to bring all things in the heavens and on earth into one under Christ's headship" (Ephesians 1:10).

23.

Wholeness as an Ideal
The symbol of the Virgin

The best way I know to draw all the parts of this book together is to focus on a symbol, one that presents in visible form and combines under one image all that we have been talking about in these pages. Since the whole book is about the fullness of graced human living, with an emphasis on sexual living, that symbol will have to be a person, and one whose very being speaks to us of life, of grace and of sexuality.

For many centuries, Christians have found such a symbol in Mary, the Virgin Mother of God. Mary is Mother of Christ, who gives life to the world. She is "full of grace" and a model to us of total, graced response to the word of God. And as the Virgin, Mary speaks of sexual purity, sexual integrity.

But Mary the Virgin stands for more than purity. Her virginity was a total wholeness, a total togetherness of soul and body. She was not only intact in a sexual sense—the *virgo intacta*—she was also intact in everything she did. As virgin "full of grace" she was whole and entire on all the levels of her being—physical, cultural, personal and transcendent—in her every action.

Virginity in Mary includes more than its sexual reality; it was for her and is for us a total human and spiritual reality. Mary the Virgin stands for undivided, graced human nature acting with wholeness and integrity, without any division or fragmentation, in every personal response.

The failure to understand this—a failure for which a lot of spiritual writers, teachers and preachers must share the blame—has led many people in our times to reject Mary as a symbol of integral Christian living. Several married people have stated to me that Mary cannot be a model for them, since sexual relations were not a part of her life and are such a significant element of their own.

Mary the Virgin somehow became for some Christians an anti-sex symbol, which is the exact opposite of what she ought to be. The most characteristic thing about Mary, after all, was the very sexual reality of carrying Christ within her womb and giving him birth between her legs. She nursed him at her breast as any mother would and raised him as any mother raises her child.

She was also a wife. She knew what it was to live with a man, adapt to his ways, and strive with him to arrive at mutual understanding.

But all of this is unfortunately overshadowed

302

in our consciousness by the fact she was a virgin; she never experienced sexual intercourse. How can married people, or those who intend to be married, relate to Mary as a symbol and model of their whole lives when she never engaged in an activity which is so much a part of married Christian life?

Virginity as an ideal

I believe that if we understand what the ideal of virginity really means, we will understand Mary to be relevant, not only to sexual purity before marriage, but to total sexual fulfillment within marriage itself. Then she can be the symbol we are looking for.

Without arguing the point, I would submit that virginity as an ideal means much more than just the physical, historical fact that a given individual—male or female—has never had sexual intercourse.

The fact of physical virginity—virginity in its precise, technical sense—is for us a symbol or sign of virginity in a much broader sense, one that goes beyond the dictionary definition. The virginity which we hold up as an ideal is more like a total state of soul than a simple biological condition.

Let us start by defining virginity: Virginity as an ideal stands for personal wholeness and intactness. The virgin is a person who acts as a total, undivided whole, without division or fragmentation, in every human act; someone who is "all together" as a person in everything he or she does.

We don't think of five-year-olds as being virgins because they have nothing to be virginal about. Nor would we really say that a lusty, sexy, loose-moraled 17-year-old boy or girl who is ready and willing to engage in every form of sexual experience short of intercourse itself is a virgin in the value-sense that this word carries for us. To be a virgin says something about one's *person*.

If we look more closely at what virginity means for us as an ideal we will immediately recognize two things: Virginity isn't always and irretrievably lost when someone falls into intercourse prior to marriage; and through marriage itself virginity should not be lost at all but brought to its fulfillment.

To be perfectly virgin in an ideal sense is to act without diminishment on all four levels of human life at once: the physical, the cultural, the personal and the graced. If we understand virginity this way, then in the measure that any part of our being—body or emotions, intellect, will, or religion—is left out of the responses we make to life, to other persons, and to God, in that same measure we fall short of the ideal of virginity. Virginity is an active and harmonious oneness of all that we are.

If this is what virginity means, then the "cold fish" concept of a virgin is a contradiction in terms. Virginity calls for total, warm, spontaneous, passionate oneness with one's body as with every other part of one's being.

I personally hold it as a logical conclusion of faith that if the Virgin Mary had in fact been called to a married life with Joseph that included sexual relations, he would have found her to be the most passionate woman alive.

It stands to reason. If Mary was perfectly virgin, then she was perfectly one with her body. To be one with the body means to express oneself in and through the flesh without any hindrance, inhibitions, or reserves. There was no love that Mary could have felt in her heart that would not have found total, spontaneous expression in the response of her body in sex. And this is what it means to be passionate where sexual expression is concerned.

"Losing" virginity?

If what virginity really stands for is the total wholeness and integrity of the person in everything one does, then no one starts life as a virgin. Virginity is not just a static fact one is born with and tries to preserve until marriage. Virginity, as we are describing it here, is a dynamic, inspiring ideal. It is something we work towards. It is the goal of perfect wholeness in everything we do. We are not born virgins; a virgin is something we try to become.

For this reason no one can totally lose virginity in one irreversible act.

It is true that physical virginity can be lost this way. And I do not want to minimize in any way the importance of coming to marriage without previous experience of sexual intercourse. The first act of giving oneself physically to another is a unique experience; it is one which spouses should share with each other. It is not always the ecstatic rapture people hope it will be, and no one should expect it to come off with no hitch at all. But it is still a special moment of discovery—of oneself, of the other person, and of sexuality itself—that is best experienced with the person with whom one will share the rest of one's life.

But many people do lose their physical virginity before marriage. Does this mean that the ideal of which we are speaking in this chapter is totally lost to them? Can one act of intercourse when we are young, or drunk, or carried away by passion, cost us an integrity of body and soul that is irretrievable? I think not.

First of all, there is nothing we can lose by sin which cannot be restored by grace. Jesus is presented all through the Gospels as the healer of human nature. And it is not just coincidence that the English words *whole* and *healthy* come from the same root. Jesus the healer restores us to health by restoring us to wholeness. But the wholeness or intactness of our human natures in everything we do is precisely the ideal of virginity which we are talking about.

Since this kind of virginity is something we never completely possess but are constantly striving for, we can never completely lose it in one act or lose it irretrievably. And for this same reason Mary the Virgin remains a model and a symbol for our hopes no matter how sinful we may at times feel ourselves to be. She already is what we are striving to become. She is proof of its possibility, a sign of God's willingness and power to bring us there.

Is virginity lost in marriage?

It seems strange to speak of anything being lost through an act for which the body was made. The human body was designed to have intercourse in marriage. People who marry, therefore, are not losing any part of their sexual endowment, but bringing it to fulfillment.

If we continue to define virginity as we have been in this chapter, we must say that the act of intercourse in marriage does not diminish virginity but increases it; does not make one less a virgin but more.

In the act of intercourse in marriage, a man or woman's whole being is able to say yes simultaneously in love. In intercourse the body is saying yes, the emotions are saying yes, the intellect is saying yes, the will is saying yes, and God himself is saying yes with both partners through his Spirit who dwells in the heart of each one. On every level of their being, when a husband and wife have intercourse together, they are saying yes to one another.

Seen this way, what takes place on the wedding night is not, as the old and unfortunate English term would have us call it, a "deflowering." It is rather the flowering of virginity. In one peak moment of wholeness everything in bride and groom is speaking simultaneously a word of surrender and love.

If we understand virginity this way it is not a negative concept. Those who intend to remain virgins until marriage are not just preserving something or holding something back. Much less are they denying their sexuality. What they are really doing is insisting that their sexuality be whole. They are saying that until their sexual response can be whole and entire—a response not just of body and emotions, but of approving intellect, committed will, and of their graced and consecrated reality as the body of Christ on earth all at the same time—they will not fragment themselves

307

as persons by responding with just part of what they are. They are saying no to partial sex out of a passionate insistence on the whole.

Saying yes to wholeness

For anyone who understands virginity in the sense we give the word here, the conflict involved in being pure is not between our sexuality and ourselves, but between partial sex and integral sex. Any temptation to be impure is an attack, not of sexuality against the integrity of our persons, but of one or the other element of sexual expression against the integral wholeness of sexuality itself. The real challenge is not to keep our sexuality in check; it is to keep it together.

Outside of marriage virginity in sexual response means a total refusal to say yes with only a part of oneself. Unless one is able to say yes intellectually and spiritually as well as emotionally, virginity says no with a passionate love for integrity.

In marriage, on the other hand, to give one's body in sex is according to the design of nature as reason understands it. When the will is totally committed to the other, and all of one's religious belief is expressed in this act of self-giving that is holy and blessed by God, then virginity requires one to hold nothing back.

The person who acts as a whole, who is "all together" in everything he or she does, will not be hung up or inhibited in the act of sex in marriage. The virgin who says yes will say it with everything at once.

In other words, virginity means passionate

purity outside of marriage, and pure passion inside of marriage.

A virgin, then, never really says no to anything, except in saying yes to wholeness. The ideal of virginity is not to be divided. And this ideal remains the same whether one is married or not.

Even the vowed, physical virginity of religious priests and sisters is a way of saying yes. The vow of celibacy is simply a radical way of affirming in faith the Christian belief that God has drawn near in Jesus Christ. The celibate renounces marriage as a way of saying in real language that he or she believes it is possible to have with Jesus Christ, here and now in this life, a relationship of friendship and love that is as real, as satisfying, and as helpful to our development as loving persons as the relationship with another human person in marriage would be. Physical sexual relations are not part of the celibate's life; but the love and commitment which are expressed by physical sex in marriage are the heart and soul of the celibate's life. And the gift of the body in celibacy is a physical way of expressing spousal consecration to Christ.

Virginity, then, or keeping ourselves whole and entire in all that we say and do, is the note on which we end. Virginity understood this way is an ideal of sexual behavior whose realization prepares us for marriage and continues to grow within marriage.

We have not offered in these pages any negative ideal of sex. We have not proposed some point at which to draw the line in our sexual experiences before marriage, as if the best Jesus Christ had to offer were a set of brakes. The question we have asked is not the negative one of where sexual activity should stop before marriage, but whether it should begin at all.

We have maintained throughout this book that all properly sexual activity is by its very nature a language of committed marital love. What we have proposed is an ideal of understanding the nature and value of this language and of keeping it authentic. No truly sexual word can have the meaning it is meant to convey outside of the actual, committed relationship of marriage. And so in the name of sexuality itself we reserve those words— all of them—for the person we eventually will marry.

In embracing this ideal we are embracing the fullness of life on all levels: physical, cultural, personal and transcendent. Our sexuality is too much a part of our being for us to diminish its reality without diminishing our humanity itself.

Sex on a purely physical level is unworthy of human beings. Simply to follow our culture and conform to the standards of our peer group in our sexual behavior is to lose ourselves as persons. To be ruled only by the goal of solitary, subjective personhood, however, is to fall into the damning isolation of pride.

We need, therefore, to find the fullness of human life by surrendering ourselves to life on a higher level: the level of the truth and goodness of God. In Jesus, the Master of the Way, teacher and healer of human life, we find the truth that sets us free and the strength that empowers us to be whole.

Admittedly, the ideals of this book are high.

But this book has been written, as we explained in the Introduction, partly as a counterbalance to those who are speaking and writing today as if teenagers had no power of free choice, no ability to understand and respond to rational ideals and to arguments based on meaning and value. I think this book appeals to free choice.

We have gone beyond free choice, however; far beyond rational meaning and values. We have proposed an ideal of perfect freedom, of total wholeness and integrity in sex that is realizable only by grace. We do not pretend that anyone can believe in, embrace, or live by the ideals and principles of this book in our society unless the Spirit of Christ move that person from within to break radically with the attitudes and values of our culture. We have need of the grace of Jesus Christ.

But that grace is available. And Mary is proof of it. The Virgin full of grace is visible evidence that a human being who is no more God than we are can be perfectly whole and entire, perfectly free in responding to the fullness of life offered by Jesus Christ without diminishment or division.

In Mary the beauty of this response is made flesh in the body and person of a woman, just as the beauty of grace itself—of the union of the divine and the human in one man—is made flesh in Jesus Christ. The concrete reality of Mary, her visible image, expresses better than any number of words all that we have tried to say. If we look to her, she will inspire us.

We still need proof, however, that we in our day, we who are neither incarnate grace as Jesus is nor full of grace like Mary, can realize in our own lives the beauty of this ideal, the beauty of a growing approximation to perfect wholeness and freedom.

For this we must be saints for one another. We must embody visibly to one another in our own flesh the strength of Jesus Christ, the wholeness of Mary the Virgin. We who are the body of Christ on earth are called and empowered by grace to become for one another "the very holiness of God" (2 Corinthians 5:27).

And that is the good news about sex.